ANGEL PRAYERS

HARNESSING THE HELP OF HEAVEN TO CREATE MIRACLES

KYLE GRAY

HAY HOUSE

Carlsbad, California • New York City • London • Sydney
Johannesburg • Vancouver • Hong Kong • New Delhi

First published and distributed in the United Kingdom by:
Hay House UK Ltd, Astley House, 33 Notting Hill Gate, London W11 3JQ
Tel: +44 (0)20 3675 2450; Fax: +44 (0)20 3675 2451
www.hayhouse.co.uk

Published and distributed in the United States of America by:
Hay House Inc., PO Box 5100, Carlsbad, CA 92018-5100
Tel: (1) 760 431 7695 or (800) 654 5126
Fax: (1) 760 431 6948 or (800) 650 5115
www.hayhouse.com

Published and distributed in Australia by:
Hay House Australia Ltd, 18/36 Ralph St, Alexandria NSW 2015
Tel: (61) 2 9669 4299; Fax: (61) 2 9669 4144
www.hayhouse.com.au

Published and distributed in the Republic of South Africa by:
Hay House SA (Pty) Ltd, PO Box 990, Witkoppen 2068
Tel/Fax: (27) 11 467 8904
www.hayhouse.co.za

Published and distributed in India by:
Hay House Publishers India, Muskaan Complex, Plot No.3, B-2,
Vasant Kunj, New Delhi 110 070
Tel: (91) 11 4176 1620; Fax: (91) 11 4176 1630
www.hayhouse.co.in

Distributed in Canada by:
Raincoast, 9050 Shaughnessy St, Vancouver BC V6P 6E5
Tel: (1) 604 323 7100; Fax: (1) 604 323 2600

Text © Kyle Gray, 2013

Ten per cent of Kyle's royalties from the sale of this book will be donated to the Scottish Society for the Prevention of Cruelty to Animals (Scottish SPCA), a charity close to his heart that receives no government funding and relies solely on public donations.

A catalogue record for this book is available from the British Library.

ISBN: 978-1-78180-151-2

Printed and bound in Great Britain by TJ International, Padstow, Cornwall.

MIX
Paper from
responsible sources
FSC® C013056

This book is dedicated to the animals of our planet, who sometimes don't have a voice. Thank you, angels, for supporting them on their journey!

∾ CONTENTS ∾

Part III: Directory of Prayers

∼ PREFACE ∼

Prayer is universal. Every religion or belief system incorporates one form of prayer or another. People pray every day for health, abundance, success or even for their crops to do well. Prayer is a daily routine for many and the last resort for others. Whatever the reason, many of us, if not all, will admit that at some point in our lives we've prayed to heaven for assistance.

I've had the pleasure of meeting many souls whose prayers have resulted in miracles, and I've known many more who feel their prayers haven't been answered at all. So many of these people are lost and bewildered because the angels and higher powers they had so much faith in didn't help them.

So, why aren't prayers answered? Is there something we've overlooked? Is there a special way of praying that creates results? This book explores exactly that, and you'll be shocked when you realize what you've been missing the whole time.

Join me in my new discovery and learn to use your prayers not only to benefit your health and wealth, but also to strengthen your connection to your life purpose, to angels and to all the blessings around you.

Your guardian angel is with you right this second, waiting for the invitation to help you in all areas of your life. As you apply this prayer technique to your daily practice and acknowledge the angelic presence in your life, I know miracles will begin to take place.

I've taught angel prayers to non-believers, absolute sceptics and people who have prayed in a certain way for decades, with astounding results. You are a creative expression of the universe, with the power to do anything. Allow angel prayers to support you on your amazing journey.

✨ ACKNOWLEDGEMENTS ✨

I'd like to thank my mum, Diane Gray, who has been a huge support to me all my life. You're my Earth angel and I'm so thankful that I've had you as a mother. Thank you for running the day-to-day business of Kyle Gray UK and believing in the powers that be. I love you!

I'd also like to say thanks to my dad. Many say I'm your mirror image, so thanks for the handsome looks and the hot head. Thanks, too, for believing in me and reminding me that I can't work 24/7!

Special thanks to Clare Hulton, my agent. You were definitely sent to me by angels; you've believed in my ideas (even when they've seemed a bit out there) and have been really patient with my sometimes last-minute approach.

I love you, Carolyn Thorne, Jo Burgess, Michelle Pilley and all at Hay House UK. You guys are amazing! I feel that I've found my spiritual home and you are my spiritual family! Huge love to the editorial team, especially if my punctuation was off!

Thanks to Leigh Fergus, who has not only become a dear friend but also a mentor. You've taught me so much about myself, about being an author and about always speaking with integrity. You're a Reiki angel and are here to teach many people how to organize themselves, ha, ha!

Special thanks to Diane Etherson, my soul sister, who is always there to listen to my somewhat crazy ideas and understand them when maybe others don't!

I'd also like to give a big shout to my amazing friends: Teri, Jennifer, Amanda, Heather, Scott, Ryan, Jonny, Toni, Ayden, John, Drew, Olivia, Andrew, Lauren, Ross and Sean! You guys are brilliant and I believe in you all!

Only love.

Namaste.

✌ PROLOGUE ✌

I'll never forget the first time I prayed to God for help. Our dog, Tora, a West Highland terrier I loved very much, had fallen ill. He'd been attacked by a neighbour's dog and his health had deteriorated rapidly. After several visits to the animal hospital, he still wasn't improving. As my dad got ready to take him to the vet yet again, he encouraged me to say goodbye to him, as he might not be coming home.

I hugged my beloved dog and patted his head. I remember thinking, *I don't want to lose you, Tora. I need you.*

My mum and dad had adopted Tora in 1986, around two years before I was born. My mum had been desperate for a dog and my dad had thought it would be a good thing, so they'd driven down from Glasgow to Ayrshire on the southwest coast of Scotland and had instantly fallen in love with the little white fur ball they'd picked up that day. They'd named him Tora after Tora-Kai, the style of karate my dad followed.

Tora was a special dog, full of character and loved by everyone. My nana, who was allergic to dogs, even wore a dust mask so she could enjoy his company.

This amazing dog even caught up on the news from time to time. There's an old black-and-white photo of him reading the local newspaper.

When I was a baby, Tora would sit by my cot as if to guard me. It was as if he was taking on the role of a big brother, looking after the baby of the family. And our connection was strong from that time on....

Now, watching Dad put Tora, wrapped in a tartan blanket, onto the back seat of our car, I asked, 'Do you think he'll come back, Mum? Do you think he'll be okay?'

'I don't know. I really hope so!' my mum said, beginning to fill up with emotion. 'Go and watch TV, son, while I cook dinner.'

I settled down in my favourite spot in front of the TV. But as my mum went into the kitchen I got down on my knees and prayed: 'Dear God, please bring back Tora. Please let him be okay. I love him very much! Amen.'

Within an hour my dad returned without Tora. He'd been put to sleep. I remember crying in the hall with my parents. I'll never forget thinking, *I wish God could have helped Tora.*

Now that my eyes are open to God's love, I realize my prayers *were* answered. Tora *was* okay. He went to his real home: he went to heaven.

PART I

THE MIRACLE
OF PRAYER

❧ 1 ❧

THE POWER OF PRAYER

'Prayer does not fit us for the greater work;
prayer is the greater work.'

Oswald Chambers

A prayer is defined as 'a solemn request for help or expression of thanks addressed to God or a higher power.' It's the moment we call out for help, seek change, need an answer or even a miracle. It's when we allow in the assistance of a power greater than ourselves or realize that power is within us.

Prayer, like angels, transcends religion. It raises our thoughts to the divine. It connects us to the love of God.

God, for me, is an energy with many names – the energy that runs through us all and makes everything one. Although my early connections were to Christian and Spiritualist churches, I see God as a universal energy. I will frequently interchange the terms 'God', 'the universe' and 'life' in this book. Whatever you call this energy, it's there to support you and guide you throughout your life.

We've all prayed to God at one time or another. Yet many of us can't explain what our prayers do or where we learned to pray. For me, prayer is metaphysical medicine. It allows me to be supported by the ultimate support. It's the moment I allow my angels to guide me, the moment I allow the will of God to direct me instead of my own.

During the planning of this book, I prayed to heaven for guidance. After surrendering to the flow of this higher power, I went to bed with the metaphysical text *A Course in Miracles*. I've been a student of this spiritual psychotherapy course for many years on and off and read the book many times, but as I began to read it yet again, it felt as though God was speaking to every cell of my being. Here's what I read:

> *'Prayer is the medium of miracles. Prayer is the natural communication of the created with the Creator. Through prayer love is received, and though miracles love is expressed.'*

My whole body was covered in goosebumps, or as I like to call them, 'angelbumps'! And it's true:

*Prayer not only brings answers, it also brings
a sense of peace, raises our awareness
and expresses love – and nothing is more
important than that.*

Prayer has always been a huge part of my life. From around the age of four I went to Sunday school at my Aunt June's church near our home in Port Glasgow. I loved going there and learning about God and how much he loved me. I also attended Boys Brigade, an interdenominational Christian youth organization that encouraged obedience, self-discipline and respect. In both of these clubs, we would open and close our meetings with prayer. Soon, starting and ending the day with prayer became a regular part of my life.

When I was young, I used to pray for toys I wanted. When I received them, I thought, *Wow, I made this happen and all I did was ask God*. But there were also times when it seemed that my prayers weren't answered – like the time Tora was put to sleep. I believed in God, but I just didn't understand Him.

Still, I used prayer to manifest things I wanted. Once my dad took me to Edinburgh Zoo and first we went to my favourite fast-food restaurant. There was a wishing well there and Dad handed me some loose change to throw into it to make wishes. As I threw each of the coins into the pool, I said inwardly, 'Please, God, let me have a good day and loads of new toys!' Selfish, I know, but I was only about six years old. And it did turn out to be an amazing day and my dad did buy me loads of new toys, including an inflatable elephant I loved.

It was in later years that I came to realize the true power of prayer. Prayer can move mountains. I've also discovered that it's an amazing way of expressing gratitude.

When working privately with clients and audiences, I've recommended prayers, and the results have often been completely astounding. To give just one example, I recently conducted an angel reading for a lovely lady named Violet. I didn't know anything about her other than she was from Fife and in her late fifties. As usual, I instructed her not to feed or prompt me with information. Then, through a prayer, I connected to her angels and loved ones on the other side.

As the reading developed, her angels told me she'd been having bad dreams that caused her to wake up during the night. They were caused by soaking up other people's negativity. People were coming to her for help all the time and she wasn't always psychically protecting herself, and therefore the energy surrounding her was turning into nightmares.

Violet admitted she woke up through the night. I suggested a few angel prayers she could use and told her to get in touch over the coming weeks to let me know how she was getting on. Here's a copy of the message she sent me:

> 'Kyle, you gave me an angel prayer to say at night. I have used it every night since. I am not up between four and five. I sleep like a log... I have not slept like this for years.... Thank you once again!'

The power of prayer can be absolutely astonishing, but in a way it's quite natural: because we're connecting with the divine, we're encouraging changes – even miracles – to occur.

So, stop for a moment and think. The last time you fell on your knees and prayed for help, did it work? Have you ever had a prayer answered? Has a situation ever miraculously resolved itself after you called on heaven for help? What about when a prayer *wasn't* answered? Why do you think that happened?

All of these issues will become important as we delve further into prayer and the world of angels.

For now, just take a few deep breaths and say to yourself:

> *'Thank you, angels, for reminding me of your presence!'*

Will they remind you? Just keep a note of any signs you receive over the next few days. These may appear as conversations, music, feathers in random places, dreams or even a visit from your guardian angel! Keep an open mind and your eyes peeled....

A Reminder from Heaven

Just to give you an idea of how angels remind us of their divine presence, here's something that happened to me recently.

I was in London on business and decided to extend my trip for a few days so that I could catch up with some friends. I'd known one of them, Jonny, since our teenage years. He's almost four years younger than I am, but our interest in music had brought us together and after that we'd formed a brotherly bond and, well, were definitely known for getting into trouble (nothing too serious!) and pushing our pranks too far.

Now we were making our way to the top of a big red bus that was going to take us to the Natural History Museum. Only a handful of people were on board, so we sat at the front on adjacent seats so that we each had two seats to ourselves. We were laughing as we talked about how things had changed and how grown up we'd become.

'You always told me that I'd be living in London before I was 21!' Jonny said. 'And here we are, on a bus together here!'

He paused for a moment.

'You know,' he went on, 'I really believe in angels. It's amazing how they can help us.'

'Yes,' I replied, 'it really is amazing how much of an influence they are in my life. I speak to them at every available opportunity, pray every morning and just love the signs they send me! Why don't we thank them for reminding us of their presence now and see what signs they bring us today?'

Both of us mentally spoke to the angels and thanked them for reminding us of their presence and sending us a sign.

Our conversation drifted from topic to topic as the bus made its way through the city streets, and then the oddest thing happened. A very elderly lady, wearing black and carrying quite a large handbag, came and sat between us, right next to Jonny. There were so many empty seats around us, so it was strange that she should have chosen to sit there.

Jonny and I looked across at each other, and Jonny just shrugged and smiled his cheeky smile.

'Hello, there,' I said to the lady. 'Would you like to swap seats so you have a seat on your own? It's just that he and I,' I pointed to Jonny, 'are together and it will let you have more space.'

'Okay, that'll be great!' she said in a European accent I couldn't place, looking at me with piercing blue eyes.

I stood up, allowed her to take my seat, then sat down beside my friend.

Then she made an 'oh' sound.

As we looked at her, she opened her hands to reveal a butterfly. 'What'll I do with this?' she asked.

'Here, give it to me, I'll put it out of the window,' I said.

'Please don't kill it! It has to live!' she said.

I took the butterfly and set it free through the open window of the bus. I looked over to the lady and smiled, saying, 'I couldn't have killed it – I'm a vegetarian, ha, ha!'

'I'm a vegan,' she replied.

She seemed to be an interesting woman. 'So, where are you off to today?' I asked. 'We're on our way to the museum to see the crystals and rocks. I'm so excited!'

'I'm going to the park to sit among the trees to get some real oxygen,' she replied. 'I do it every day, as the air isn't the same when you're in the city. Then I'm going to church to pray. It's very important that you believe in God and His angels. You have to know they're with you! For many years I lost my faith and I felt lost. Now I have it back, I know it's more important than ever.'

Jonny and I looked at each other open-mouthed. There was our reminder from the angels!

Could they have inspired this lady to sit beside us? Was she a messenger from heaven? We couldn't stop thinking about it all day.

After our trip to the museum, we went shopping before heading back home on a bus that was absolutely crammed with people. We squeezed in downstairs and stood holding on to the rail until after about three or four stops at least 20 people got off the upper deck and we were able to go up there and sit in two adjacent aisle seats.

We were just planning on picking up Chinese food for dinner when I felt a tap on my shoulder.

'*No way, no way, no way!*' Jonny was saying at the top of his voice.

The lady we'd met was on the seat directly behind us!

She looked at us both and said simply, 'There are no coincidences in life – only Godincidences!'

Then she pushed the button to stop the bus and made her way downstairs.

I remember looking out of the window as the bus pulled away to see my new friend looking up and waving to us.

Angels certainly sent that lady to us. Through synchronicity and a perfectly orchestrated series of events, they reminded us of their presence.

≈ 2 ≈

PRAYING TO ANGELS

'We should pray to the angels, for
they are given to us as guardians.'

St. Ambrose

Angels are always with us. Our guardian angel has been with us from the day we were born and will be with us until we return to heaven. This divine being looks at us with the eyes of unconditional love. No judgement, no expectations — all they see when they look at us is the potential to create a magnificent life.

Angels are mentioned in every main Abrahamic religion (Christianity, Judaism and Islam), but these formless spiritual beings also feature in most other belief systems, albeit under different names. Buddhism and Hinduism speak about Devas, beings that can move through the air speedily and are only seen and heard by those with extrasensory powers; while in the Japanese Shinto religion, the divine beings described as Kami have many similarities with angels, and many Native American traditions speak about the 'star ancestors' and the 'sky people'.

Seeing Angels

Angels not only remind us of their presence, they also show themselves to us. One of the most fascinating things I've found out about them is that they'll always do this in a way we understand. So some people see angels in traditional form, with wings, while others see them as elongated humans with bright lights around them, or even just as orbs of energy.

Whatever their form, they'll come to us in a way that makes us feel comfortable and loved. When I think about angels or invite them to draw close, I get a picture of them in my mind. Occasionally I'll see them physically, but mostly it's as if they're projecting a picture of themselves in front of me or the client I'm working with. They usually look similar to celebrities and public figures. This is so that people can relate to them. For example, my guardian angel, Kamael, looks like President Obama (I've seen him physically on a number of occasions now), whereas my mother sees hers as looking similar to Oliver Cromwell. It's fascinating what angels will do to make themselves recognizable to us!

Don't worry if you don't see angels physically; just imagine them and they'll guide your thoughts to them....

Angels Are Friends!

Over the years I've been working with these phenomenal beings, they've become my friends. I enjoy sharing their company.

Our guardian angel is a perfect friend who will support us when we're down, listen to us vent when we have to or join us as we dance to our favourite song. When I was working as a DJ, it never surprised me when I saw angels dancing, too. Angels are joyful beings; they love nothing more than having fun with us!

Facets of God's Love

Angels follow one code: *love*. They are the creations of divine love and want nothing other than for us to find peace and happiness. They can only help us, however, when we give them permission to do so.

One of the greatest gifts we have been given is free will. Everything in life is a choice – where to go, what to do, how to react, how to interact, how to ask heaven for help.... Most of us try and fight things out on our own, but when we invite angels into our life, we allow them to take our burdens and lovingly direct us to a place where we feel safe.

*A prayer is that moment when we allow
heaven to support us in our endeavours.*

It's really important to mention that this book is *not* encouraging you to worship angels over God. The reason for this is that angels are God's creation — they are facets of God's love. Working with them, connecting to their energy, brings us closer to God.

God is universal — the energy goes beyond gender, status and worship. God is connected to all living things. God is the universe, the sky, the land, the blood that flows through our veins. God is everywhere. One of my favourite people on Earth, Rev. Run, says, 'God is love', and he's absolutely right.

Take a deep breath and acknowledge your creator's presence by saying:

'God is love.
I am love.
We are love.'

All this love means the universe wants us to be supported. It wants us to receive abundance because it's abundant; it wants us to receive love because it's loving. There's unlimited energy and support out there for us. When we pray for help, we're not depriving anyone else of that help — *there's enough for everyone.*

'There's enough for everyone' is one of my favourite affirmations.

So many people don't want to pray for help, or feel that their situation is too trivial for angels to bother with. Please remember that your happiness is *not* trivial – and it's not 'unspiritual' either. Spiritual growth is about creating heaven on Earth – it's about creating bliss, abundance, connectedness, safety and love. Angels can help us with this. They *want* to help us.

Connecting with Angels

If you've never worked with angels before, then there's a couple of different ways you can speak to them.

I speak to angels as a force, and calling on them using the general term 'angels' is absolutely perfect, because there's an angel for almost everything you can imagine and the being best suited to your situation will come to your aid. The other option you have is speaking to your guardian angel. Many of my friends who follow the Catholic faith have been encouraged to do this since childhood.

You don't need any formalities for this – you can just act as if your best friend is in the room. When I speak to my guardian angel, I just chat away as normal. All you need to know is that your angel is there for you and is willing to listen – without judgement!

Of course it's nice to have a formal or specific prayer to show your respect for the universe and its creations, and the traditional Catholic prayer to your guardian angel is a beautiful one. It's short, sweet and easy to remember. I couldn't resist sharing it here:

'Angel of God,
My guardian dear,
To whom His love commits me here,
Ever this day/night
Be at my side,
To light and guard,
To rule and guide.
Amen.'

Types of Angel

You can also call on a specific type of angel. There is a hierarchy of angels similar to the ranking in a corporate workplace (*see page 71*) and the different types serve us and our planet in different ways.

Archangels

Most people have heard of archangels. These spectacular beings act as managers of the angels, if you like – they work with the guardian angels, overseeing their projects and purpose. They can be called upon by anyone at any time – they're able to be everywhere at once because, like all angels, they're multi-dimensional.

Although there are thousands of archangels, some are better known than others, and I have outlined their roles and shared their wisdom in Part II of this book.

Peace Angels

Peace angels are a collective of angels dedicated to bringing peace to our world. Whenever there is a disaster such as a war or a flood, these angels are there bringing peace to as many people as they can. They work tirelessly to comfort those who are bereaved, injured, abandoned or hurt.

Whenever I hear about a world crisis, I send peace angels to help. What's amazing about prayers for peace is that they join together to become even more powerful, so our prayers do contribute to peace.

Remember, angels cannot help unless we invite them in. The reason for this is that we have to learn to ask for help, and to learn that there's more to life than we can see. So many of us live an independent life directed by our own will, but when we pray, we open up to the divine will and allow it to support us.

Guardian Angels

Other than archangels, the angels closest to us are guardian angels. We all have our own personal guardian, but can communicate with this 'choir' of angels as a whole, too.

One of the best things about guardian angels is that we can speak to other people's guardians as well. I have done this on a number of occasions when there has been a disagreement or an awkward situation.

Try it! The next time you're faced with an argument with someone, or a situation that's upsetting or just plain difficult, speak to the other person's angel! Thank the angel for bringing peace to the situation for the highest good of all.

Ceremony Angels

Whenever a ceremony or ritual takes place, angels watch over the proceedings. Public meetings, weddings, baptisms, bar mitzvahs – you name it, angels are present.

At a baptism, no matter what the faith or religion, angels pour blessings over the child as the parents acknowledge the higher power.

Bar mitzvahs are special, too. They represent coming of age and being able to hold your own before God. Angels celebrate and come together with you, and as you acknowledge your inner strength, they do, too.

When you come together with another person in marriage, your energy is bound together before the universe. It is a magical moment! (*If you have broken away from a marriage or other ceremonial tie but still feel bound by it, however, please see archangels Michael on page 141, and Zadkiel on page 189, in the Angel Directory. They can help dissolve old bonds that hold you back.*)

Public meetings can be magical, too. I'll never forget the time I went to hear the Dalai Lama give a talk in Edinburgh. When he spoke, I saw angels all around him. Their golden light washed over the hundreds of us who were there and it felt so healing. My whole body was tingling, and I was so in awe I felt myself drifting off into a deep meditative state. It dawned on me that we were all becoming one – one mind, one energy, focusing on one thing: *peace*.

Now that you've learned more about angels, why not extend your light to them? Try the following:

© Say the traditional Catholic prayer to connect with your guardian angel (*page 18*).

© Speak to your guardian angel just as you would to a good friend. Tell your angel your concerns and know you're being heard.

© If you're concerned about a particular situation, send peace angels there.

© If you'd like to resolve some issues with a friend, colleague or family member, speak to their guardian angel and thank them for supporting the highest and best outcome for all.

© Whenever you feel fearful or need to turn around a situation, take a deep breath and affirm: 'God is love. I am love. We are love.'

3

THE MAGNITUDE OF GRATITUDE

'Gratitude bestows reverence, allowing us to encounter everyday epiphanies, those transcendent moments of awe that change forever how we experience life and the world.'

John Milton

There's something really powerful about giving thanks. Think about a time when you really went out of your way for others — you were their support, their rock, their angel. Didn't you feel fulfilled when they said the very important words *thank you*? It's exactly the same for the universe — it loves to help, and more important, it loves to be thanked.

Gratitude adds power to our prayers; it allows us to move from a place of fear to a place of appreciation.

If we're in a state of fear, denial, self-hatred or resentment, it's a different story. Then the ego can begin running the show. What is the ego? It's the voice of fear, the part of us that makes us challenge our divine intelligence. It's the part that makes us feel low and that we're not good enough.

I recently heard Dr Wayne Dyer say that 'ego' is an acronym for 'edging God out'. That totally made sense to me! The ego edges the voice of God out. It makes us feel lonely, judgemental and separate from others – and that's the last thing we want, especially if we're hoping for answers to our prayers.

By feeling grateful, however, we let God in. Then we're connected to love, and as miracles occur naturally as expressions of love, our prayers will begin to be answered.

Gratitude Opens the Heart to Receive

When we focus on our blessings and are grateful for them, it's amazing what happens to us: unconsciously, our shoulders relax and we begin to smile. When we're focusing on the negative things in our life, however, our body tenses up and we frown. Now it's a known fact that it takes more energy to frown than it does to smile!

Something else happens when we focus on gratitude: we open our heart. Not the heart that pumps blood around our body (although I wouldn't be surprised if it affects this, too), but our spiritual heart, the part of our soul that welcomes blessings into our life. By opening our heart to receive blessings, we open ourselves to a flow of support and abundance from the angels.

Angels rejoice when we give thanks. They love nothing more than seeing us content. When I give thanks, my angels dance and swirl around me.

List Five Things...

It can be just as easy to say 'thank you' and 'I love' as to say 'I don't want' and 'I hate'. I avoid the 'h' word like the plague. As soon as we use it, we're letting fear take over the show.

I once had the most amazing client called Ashley. She was a bright, shining spirit — so down to earth, but connected at the same time. At the end of the reading, we spoke about the power of gratitude and she said she encouraged it in her kids. Whenever they said they hated something, she listened, then said, 'Now tell me five things you're grateful for!'

I said, 'What an amazing idea! I have to borrow this!'

Now every time I hear people say they 'dislike' or 'hate' something, I encourage them to list five things they love! Or five things they're grateful for, or five blessings from their day.

Try it now! Close your eyes, take a few deep breaths and see if you can list five things you're grateful for. Remember, angels are listening!

Gratitude Intentions

I recently went to a high school to speak about my life and the power of angels. I took seven classes that day, ranging from 30 to over 200 students, but what I remember most was a class of just 14 teenagers who were known for their behavioural challenges. Although these were said to be the most difficult pupils, I felt drawn to speak to them because this was probably the class I'd have been in if I'd been at that school.

Mind you, the nerves did kick in when I saw a police officer in the classroom, too. This didn't faze the kids, though! I started to speak to them about creating your dreams, but most of them were more interested in making sarcastic comments. It was nearly the end of the day and I had to think fast!

A voice inside me said, 'Practise gratitude,' and it was instant inspiration.

'Right,' I said, 'so who here has a dream? Who here wants to make that dream come true?'

They all raised their hands, though most still looked as though they could hardly be bothered.

'Well, there's something that'll really focus your energy on making your dream come true! Do you know what that is? It's gratitude.'

'What's gratitude?' asked a particularly challenging young man at the front.

'For me, gratitude is being thankful for the things and people I have in my life, and of course for the things that might not even have come into my life yet!'

'What d'you mean? You're grateful for things you don't have?'

'Precisely,' I said. 'I'm grateful for the things I want to create.'

The boy thought for a moment. 'That's quite cool, actually...'

'Shall we give it a go, then?'

I asked the students to make two lists numbered one to five. The first list was the things they were grateful for in their life at that time and the second was their 'gratitude intentions', the things they were hoping to create in the future.

You could have heard a pin drop as everyone, including the police officer, wrote down their intentions.

I remember looking over one young man's shoulder as he wrote:

I'm grateful for:

1. My mum and dad.

2. My Xbox.

3. My brother's health.

4. Good friends.

5. My new trainers.

I was so pleased that he saw a family member's health as a huge blessing, but what was even better was that one of his gratitude intentions was: 'Stopping smoking.' I felt really moved that he was thinking of changing his behaviour for the better at this early stage of his life. And it goes to show that gratitude can really turn the energy around....

Acknowledge Your Blessings

It's a great practice to start every day by giving thanks. Usually I start with 'Dear God and angels, first of all I would like to thank you for all of the blessings in my life, especially...' and then I list all the things I'm thankful for that morning.

I also do it in the car, because the hour's drive to work gives me the opportunity to list all the things that are great in my life. Once I have done this, I work on the things I want to create or feel need more attention, and usually they manifest very quickly.

Recently I was running late for work. I couldn't get hold of my client to tell him I'd be late, and I really didn't like the idea of someone who'd paid a deposit to see me waiting outside my door wondering what was going on. I'd missed the fast train, so I jumped into my car and began the drive into the city.

As soon as I reached the bottom of my street, I decided to turn off my radio and begin focusing on my blessings. I reached out to the angels and said, 'Let's make this day positive! First of all, I'm so grateful for this amazing car that I'm driving safely to my place of work. I'm so grateful for my office – how cosy it is, its amazing décor and the fact that it creates a safe place for those who come to heal. I'm so grateful for you, angels, for the work we do together and for being able to connect with heaven to bring information through. I'm so grateful for my current weight loss, for my health, for my parents, for their support, for the way my mum constantly organizes me, and for my two kittens, who just exude innocence and love from their very being!'

By now I was beginning to feel excited and uplifted. I was aligning my spirit with the angels and it felt completely right.

'Thank you, angels,' I went on, 'for making sure I'm on schedule and for safely guiding me to work with no resistance or setbacks. It's so good to be in my office shining my light!'

I spoke with gratitude, as if my prayer had already been answered. Not only that, but my energy was bright and happy, and I was trusting in the angels. And... every traffic light was green, every roundabout was clear, and every place where there was normally a traffic jam was free-flowing. It was a miracle.

I turned on the radio and had to laugh, as Justin Bieber was singing about spreading wings and flying away. It felt as if the angels were sending me a message, encouraging me to spread my wings and fly alongside them through my day.

So I surrendered to the divine, counted my blessings and, amazingly, was able to get to my office with time to spare.

Gratitude Lists, Journals and Jars

There are many ways to express your gratitude. One that can become a really heartwarming experience is to create a list of *thank yous* to the universe. You can create a special book for this or just use random pieces of paper. However you do it, it can really support your growth.

I recently came across the idea of keeping a huge jar of memories – writing down a memory every day on a scrap piece of paper, a receipt or whatever else you can get your hands on and keeping them all in a jar to look at in later years. I thought it would be even better to do this with your gratitude thoughts!

As I was writing this section, I was distracted and looked at Facebook. The top post on my feed was by

Gabrielle Bernstein, author of *Spirit Junkie,* and here's what she wrote:

> *'When we put our pen to paper awesome miracles can occur. Bust out your journal and document your dreams. The universe is reading.'*

Don't you just love synchronicity?

Facebook and Twitter

The universe hears our thoughts even if they're on the internet or stored in a Word document. That's right — everything we put 'out there' is picked up by this wave of energy.

This was brought to my attention by a dream one evening in which two angels visited me and said, 'Your Facebook page becomes a vision board. Every photograph, statement and emotion you share on there is being shared with the universe!'

It makes total sense, but unfortunately so many people post all the sadness in their lives — everything from ill health to hangovers to relationship problems. When it comes to your Facebook pages, fill them with love, nice pictures and all the things you like. That way, you'll enjoy even more blessings. And then you can share your gratitude, too!

For now, why not run through these exercises?

© Start off your day with gratitude! Think of all the things you're grateful for and then think about what you'd like to be grateful for in the day ahead. For example: 'I'm grateful for a safe journey to work, I'm grateful for a good parking space, I'm grateful for positive communication today...'

© Write down all your blessings on a piece of paper or in your journal or post them on the internet or put them in a jar.

© List five blessings you already have and five blessings you'd like to create. You can do it!

~ **4** ~

THE SPIRITUAL LAW OF MANIFESTATION

'Your imagination is your preview
of life's coming attractions.'

Albert Einstein

One reason why gratitude is so important is that our imagination really does create our life. Every thought we think, every word we speak and every prayer we send contributes. It doesn't matter whether those words and thoughts contain love or fear, the universe is always responding to them through the spiritual Law of Manifestation.

Manifestation is the ability to create something in life. It can be anything from a situation to a relationship to a state of health. The one thing that's really important to know is that the Law of Manifestation is working right now.

Many people have heard of the Law of Attraction, which teaches that we attract what we focus on. The Law of Manifestation teaches that we *create* whatever we focus on, but it works in conjunction with the Law of Attraction because it creates a magnet and draws the energy of whatever we focus on to us.

So, what are you focusing on? Are you a worrier? If so, it's time to change old habits! Focus on the best possible outcome, then you'll magically manifest it. Angels can help you. Check out Jeremiel and Jophiel in the Angel Directory (*pages 117 and 123*) for support with your new positive mindset!

Manifestation and Healing

We can work with the Law of Manifestation to bring healing to our physical body. I recently had a client who was going through what I call the 'c' word – cancer – and wanted to use her thoughts to support her healing.

I loved this lady's determination. Here are some of the tips we worked on to guide her safely into remission:

Create Love in Your Body

One of the most common things we think when we're hit by dis-ease is *I'm going to fight this*. If you've ever thought like this, first of all I want to honour your wish to be healed. But the most important thing I can say is that you don't want to create a 'war' in your body by fighting your dis-ease; you want to love it until it's gone. Love is the only thing that will eradicate fear, and dis-ease is a product of fear, whether conscious or unconscious, so the way to heal is to create love in your body.

Ditch the Negative Vocabulary

When you say 'I have,' then the name of your dis-ease you are affirming it into your body. What you can do instead is replace the medical diagnosis with something uplifting. So, instead of saying, for instance, 'I have cancer,' you could say, 'My body is well and healed.'

Believe You're Already Healed

One of the greatest tools in manifesting healing is to know you're already healed. With my client I encouraged her to see herself completely healed, fit and with a full head of hair blowing in the wind. She focused on this picture so strongly that before she knew it, it was real life.

Remember That the Universe Is Vast

When it comes to manifesting a better life, through healing or whatever else, so many people think it's selfish or wrong because the energy could be going somewhere else. Remember, the universe's energy is infinite. It'll never run out. There's more than enough to go around!

Manifestation and Materialization

The Law of Manifestation will allow us to produce material abundance, too. Again, many people see this as an issue, but if we create a beautiful car to move from A to B, a gorgeous home to live in and more than enough wealth to get by, that doesn't make us unspiritual. Remember, the universe is full of abundance!

I recently met a lady who pointed out that when people manifest things, they're preventing others from creating those things. I was quick to correct her. There's more than enough for everyone, so open your heart to receive the blessings you deserve.

What are you waiting for? If you want to manifest a new job, imagine picking up your first pay slip. If you want to manifest enough money for a new washing machine, see yourself taking out a wash and smelling the divine scent of your favourite fabric softener....

Manifestation, Miracles and Magic

When people discover the spiritual power of manifestation, they often want to start changing everything in their lives that's not to their liking. While this is understandable, if we want to craft, change or mould something so it fits our lifestyle, that's magic — we're aiming to fix something external to us — and angels teach us that we're connected to everyone and everything. Therefore, for the best results, we must *be* the change — we must create miracles.

> *Looking outside ourselves for change is magic. Changing from within creates miracles.*

It's my view that we create a life of abundance when we remember we're one with God, when we've chosen to forgive and when we see that we deserve miracles because we *are* a miracle.

So, if you're ready to create a better life for yourself, here are some thoughts that will support you:

◎ Whom do you need to forgive?

◎ How do you feel about this situation?

◎ What are you grateful for?

Successful Manifestation

Take some time now to focus on what you want to manifest. Whether it is health, wealth or anything else, you can't influence or change anyone else's life but your own, so ensure your thoughts are for the highest good and focused on your path.

Visualize what you want and really feel as though it has manifested in your life. Then say this prayer in support:

'Dear angels, I am so grateful for this manifestation and for the blessings that I have received. Thank you for your support in creating them! And so it is!'

5

SURRENDER TO HEAVEN

'Prayer is not asking. Prayer is putting
oneself in the hands of God, at His
disposition and listening to His voice
in the depth of our hearts.'

Mother Teresa

Manifestation can help us create a better life, but
ultimately we are supported by the hands of God and
angels, not our own.

Also, sometimes, despite our best efforts, things
just don't change. Then we try to impose our will and
force through what we want. This is a clear sign that we
are living in fear and our ego has taken over.

One of the things that happens when our ego takes
control is that it makes us fear the unknown. We try to
prepare for every eventuality and this takes us away
from the present moment and clogs our mind with
'what ifs'. The result? Even more fear!

At this point, what we need to do is to surrender to heaven. When we do this, we let go of fear and let love in. This will lead to peace.

The dictionary definition of 'surrender' is 'cease resistance to an enemy or opponent and submit to their authority', but for me, what surrendering means is giving God and the angels control.

Trusting the Flow of Life

When we surrender to heaven, we *trust* that life is supporting us. We carry on as best we can, knowing we are being supported. And we will be supported. Our needs will be met. *Trust* that this will happen!

If you begin to get impatient and feel things aren't changing quickly enough, you're back in fear. Trust that your prayers are being answered, trust that God is taking control, trust that the miracle workers known as angels are with you and are guiding your life – including the timing.

God is never late.

Angels are never late.

Timing is always perfect.

Surrender Your Concerns

Surrendering to heaven means surrendering our concerns to heaven. It doesn't matter what they are –

issues at home, at work, in our finances or about our health – if we surrender them to heaven, angels can intervene and guide us to the answer.

If that answer isn't what we thought it would be, or what we were hoping for, that doesn't mean the process isn't working. Angels will proceed one step at a time until we're where we need to be. It's like climbing a ladder – we can only go up one rung at a time. As we take one step, another is presented. Our challenge is to recognize the steps and to thank the angels for illuminating them for us.

Prayers of Release and Surrender

When we pray, we can surrender our concerns to God or to angels. It doesn't matter which – angels are working in God's divine light and following the universal balance. Here are some prayers of surrender:

Surrender Your Health

'Divine angels of God, I surrender my wellbeing to you. Thank you for leading the way to health. I am well!'

Surrender Your Wealth

'Healing angels, I surrender my material needs to you, knowing that prosperity and wealth are with me now! And so it is!'

Surrender Your Home

'Angels of harmony, I surrender my home concerns to you, knowing your light of serenity shines on this space and all those within it.'

Surrender Your Purpose

'Angels of life, thank you for lovingly guiding my purpose so that I reach my purest potential. I surrender this to you, knowing you are showing me the way!'

Surrender Your Relationships

'Angels of love, thank you for allowing your gentle healing rays to wash over my relationships. I surrender all my concerns about those I love to you, knowing that our bond is already healed! And so it is!'

Take some time now to think of what you're ready to surrender to heaven. By thinking this over carefully, or even writing a list, you're taking steps towards a miraculous life.

Another good idea is to surrender your whole day to angels and simply allow them to guide you. Try this prayer:

'Thank you, angels, for shining your light on my day. I surrender my day to you, knowing that only good lies before me! And so it is!'

～ 6 ～

ANGEL PRAYER TECHNIQUES

'If the only prayer you said was
thank you, that would be enough.'

Meister Eckhart

I learned how to pray for help through Sunday school
and Boys Brigade and the early angel books I read. All
of these instructed me to ask for help and then look
out for the answers that would come to me. Now, I
have to say that a lot of the time that actually worked.
But I have to admit I was stumped when it didn't.

I wondered why – and then something dawned on
me. According to the Law of Manifestation, as you now
know, we create whatever we focus on. So, if we put
out a request to the universe to bring us an answer in
the future, what will we create? Waiting for an answer
in the future. That's not much help when we want our
prayers answered now.

The other thing I noticed was that when I was praying for help, I was always lacing my prayers with what I *didn't* want to happen. So I was putting power into the very situations that I was praying to be released from.

Here's a trivial situation to help you understand how this works. You're on the motorway and you're running out of petrol and there's no service station in sight. You hope the angels can help. You call out: 'Dear angels, please don't let me run out of petrol! Please let me get to the service station before I do! Thank you!'

The first thing you've done here is put the issue out into the universe. That's fine, but as you're focusing on 'running out of petrol', that's what you're putting out. You've also said the word 'please', as if you're worried that the angels *can't* help you, and you've acknowledged that the petrol *is* going to run out.

Here's how to correct this prayer: 'Divine angels, thank you so much for guiding me safely to the service station. I'm overjoyed that there's more than enough fuel to get me there! This journey has been a breeze and I'm so thankful you're here with me! And so it is!'

Do you see the difference? What *is* the difference?

Affirmative Prayer

Affirmative prayer is a metaphysical technique where instead of praying for an answer in the future, we give thanks for it as if it has already happened. The technique is simple:

- Acknowledge the angel(s) or whomever you're praying to.

- Thank them for their help.

- Affirm that the change has already happened.

- Say 'And so it is' to state that your wish has already been fulfilled.

Let's look at this in a bit more detail.

Through affirmative prayer we're acknowledging that angels are guiding us right now, we're expressing gratitude for that guidance and we're confirming we're safe. We're working with the Law of Manifestation, too, because we're affirming that angels are with us and that our situation has already been resolved.

Gratitude is an important factor, too.

With your prayers, I encourage you to let go of the word 'please' and replace it with the powerful words 'thank you'.

We don't have to plead with angels for help – they're there to help us. And the universe is so vast that there's enough energy for all of us, so we don't have to beg. If we open ourselves up to this abundance with the words 'thank you', we welcome it in now!

Affirmations

When people refer to 'affirmations', they're usually talking about the profound and positive statements that are often used to change lives. But every statement we make is an affirmation — that's everything from 'Same shit, different day' to 'I'm so hungover' to 'I've got this dis-ease.'

The point is that when we say 'I am' and then a word or phrase, we're attracting the energy of those words to us. An affirmation is a declaration to the universe that something is true, and it will listen to us and make it true. So do we really want to affirm we're hungover?

Affirmations influence how we see ourselves, and they influence how others see us, too. So if we keep affirming, 'I'm just not good enough', there's a good chance that everyone around us will take our word for it.

What we need to do is not only change our affirmations to something positive, but to place them in our prayers, too.

© Instead of saying, 'I'm so scared, angels, please protect me,' try, 'Thank you, angels, for protecting me. I feel so safe knowing you're here!'

© Instead of saying, 'God, why am I so ugly? Please help me to be beautiful,' try, 'Thank you, God and angels, for helping me discover my inner beauty and reflect it back to the world!'

© Instead of saying, 'Please, angels, help me get out of debt,' try, 'Thank you, angels, for the abundance in my life. It feels so good to get the old weight off my shoulders!'

Try it for yourself. Think about what you're constantly putting out into the universe and how it could be affecting your life.

Affirmations and Feelings

One of the statements in *The Teachings of Abraham* by Esther and Jerry Hicks, the leading authorities on the Law of Attraction, is: 'You can never be thin if you feel fat!' That really jumped out at me, so I've drawn up the following statements to help you understand even more:

© You can never be rich if you feel poor.

© You can never be healed if you feel sick.

© You can never be beautiful if you feel ugly.

© You can never be accepted if you feel rejected.

© You can never be seen if you feel invisible.

© You can never be loved if you feel hate.

It's really simple: your feelings and your prayers come together and there you are! You might be saying, 'Easier said than done,' but I have to remind you of something: that's an affirmation, too!

One further point on feelings:

Every time you invite angels to help you, notice the feelings you're giving off.

Then, if necessary, you can change them.

This is where our work on gratitude comes in handy. When we tell angels what we're grateful for, we light up our soul and to them we're a sparkle of light. We're feeling good, too, so we're ready to focus our prayers on what we want to create. Whatever it is, feel as though it has happened already!

Healing in the Now

This is especially important when it comes to healing. Healing doesn't have to be physical healing, of course – it can be the healing of a situation, a relationship or an old mindset. The point is that many of us end up hoping that the future will deliver the answer.

If we're looking beyond the present for the answer, we're not in a state of love, but fear.

What we have to do is to feel healed now, to know that healing has already taken place and to give our power to this moment, this holy instant.

Last Christmas I received a long board as a gift from my parents. If you don't know what that is, it's an extra-long skateboard that's used for picking up considerable speed, especially on downhill runs. My board wasn't built for skate parks, but being the rebel I am, I took it to one anyway.

I was doing well learning to skate with my new toy and decided to take a few downhill ramps. Before I knew it, I wanted to do three at once! Well, you know where this is going, don't you? That old saying 'crawl before you walk' comes to mind, doesn't it? But hey, I decided I was going down three ramps in one go. And then, before I even set off, I suddenly knew that it wasn't going to work. 'I'm not gonna make it, I'm not gonna make it' was my affirmation. I was setting myself up for disaster!

'Three, two, one, go!' my friends shouted as I pushed off down a 20-foot vertical ramp. As I shot down, I began to scream 'Aaaaaaah!' at the top of my lungs. That wasn't the best affirmation either.

As I hit the flat and began to take off, I realized, to my horror, that I was heading in the direction of a ramp that launched you into the air. No way, I wasn't doing that! I tried to steer my board away, but the ramp was just getting closer and closer, so I decided to put my foot down.

That was it — my ankle clicked, my knee popped and down I went.

After that it got much worse — as I lay there rolling around in agony, my best friend Scott ran towards me with a video camera and got the whole thing on film. I was mortified!

I tried to walk it off, but I knew something wasn't right. It was time to go home.

I had clients that evening and as I read for them I managed to focus my attention away from the weird twinges in my knee. But by the time I'd finished, I couldn't even stand up.

'Please, angels, heal my knee, heal my ankle. I want to let this all go!' I cried out, looking up at my bedroom ceiling.

At that moment, my mother burst through the door, saying, 'The angels have just asked me to take you to the hospital!'

After about an hour at the hospital, we were seen by a doctor. He asked me to explain what was going on.

'I'm experiencing a lot of sensations in my knee and ankle, doc,' I said.

'What do you mean by "sensations"?' he asked.

'He means pain! He doesn't believe in saying that word, but he means pain,' my mother replied.

'I speak to angels,' I explained, 'and they've just told me I've ruptured the ligaments in my knee and ankle. Can I just have crutches, please?'

'We'll have to do some assessments, take an X-ray and see if those angels are right then,' the doctor replied, looking puzzled.

I went through a number of exercises wearing one of those hospital nightgowns and then waited for another hour.

Finally the doctor came in to say, 'You were right – you've ruptured your ligaments! You'll be off your feet for a couple of weeks. We recommend crutches, and if you want, we can prescribe some painkillers. You should be back to normal in four to six weeks.'

'I'll take the crutches, you take the painkillers and I'll be walking again by Monday!' I told him.

He just laughed.

In spite of my bravado, when I went home with my crutches I was in fear, hoping the future would bring the answer. I wasn't acknowledging the here and now. It was time to work with Archangel Raphael and his healing angels. It was time to affirm that the healing had already happened.

I repeated the following prayer over and over again, believing every word:

> *'Divine angels and Archangel Raphael, thank you for the healing that has already been given to my knee and ankle. I am free and flowing! And so it is!'*

I remember falling asleep that night visualizing a green and golden light washing away any stuck or old energy in my body.

The next day I didn't take any chances — I relaxed in bed all day, catching up on my favourite TV shows and going through a workbook on chakras (*for more on angels and chakras, see Metatron, page 129*). All through the day I kept repeating the prayer.

The next day I was walking perfectly again. We passed the crutches on to someone who needed them!

Prayers and Affirmations

Why not get some paper now and take the time to rethink how you say your prayers? If you've been praying for something in the hope that it will arrive in the future, start thanking heaven for it as if it has already arrived.

Another great thing would be to replace every negative statement you make with a positive affirmation. My favourite is 'The angels surround my day with love!' This is easy to remember and will definitely realign your thoughts with the 'good stuff'.

∽ 7 ∾

THE SPIRITUAL LAW OF GRACE

'But what we can do, as flawed as we are, is still see God in other people and do our best to help them find their own grace. That's what I strive to do, that's what I pray to do every day.'

Barack Obama

So, we can use affirmative prayer to pray for ourselves, but what about others? Here we'll look at how the Law of Grace can transmute our debts both emotionally and physically, heal relationships and allow us to pray for others without causing any karma.

Grace is defined as 'simple elegance' or 'refined movement'. It is an essence that moves through us all. It's the part of our divine intelligence that searches for a better way. It's the part that guides us from pain to healing, from past to present, from fear to love.

Do you ever remember being in the middle of an argument, feeling your blood boil and then, just as you're about to explode, hearing a voice saying, 'Don't do this. You don't need to do this. Walk away.' That's grace.

Have you ever offered to carry an elderly lady's luggage, or said 'Bless you' to someone sneezing in the street, or offered a tissue to a person who's feeling emotional? That's grace, too.

Grace is a quality of spirit, and spirit is love. When we align ourselves with love, we allow ourselves to be guided by grace. Grace helps us heal others and resolve problems. It is the light of the angels, the love of God's creation, the silent and still voice that comforts us all.

We open ourselves to grace through forgiveness, or when we help others. We live a life of grace when we focus on our blessings. When we are full of grace, we grow energetic wings that carry us forward.

Here's a prayer for bringing grace into your life:

'Thank you, angels of grace, for blessing my life with your presence! I stand with poise and integrity, being the best I can be. And so it is.'

Sending Healing Prayers of Grace

If we pray for others, of course we're performing a great deed, but it may not help them and could also have some karmic consequences for us. If we're sending healing to people and they haven't learned their spirituals lesson from that particular situation, the energy can come back to us and create some blocks for us, too. Or, if we're sending healing to an argument between two friends, we could be preventing them from learning lessons about creating harmony. This, in turn, could create another lesson for us.

The Law of Grace, however, is the one law that can overrule the Law of Karma. It's the spiritual law that allows us to send love to others and pray for them in the hope that our prayers penetrate their souls and bring them the help they deserve.

When we pray under the Law of Grace, we prohibit any karma or unnecessary blocks from coming back to us. If we pray for others and their soul really requires that healing, it can accept it for them and override their ego and fears. All we have to do at the end of our prayer is say 'under the Law of Grace' or 'in the Law of Grace' to ensure it happens.

In my Reiki training, I learned something similar: that we can't send healing to others unless they ask or allow us to do so. In general, having permission is always best, but in an emergency, the Law of Grace will ensure the angels can intervene if they are able.

Welcoming in the Angels of Grace

When something goes wrong or we don't know what to do, we can invite in the angels of grace and allow them to direct us to the best possible solution. When we pray for someone, or for the resolution of a particular situation, they will send waves of healing light, bringing peace and harmony to everyone involved.

The next time you find yourself in a situation where you don't know what to do, welcome the angels of grace, welcome God, make room for miracles and you'll be amazed by the help you'll be given.

Situations like this can arise at any moment. Recently I went to my friend Karen's house to have lunch and get my hair done. She's a session stylist who has worked for the stars and she'd offered to create a modern new look for me. I'm also friends with her daughter, Ayden, who is around the same age as I am, so we'd decided to all meet up at the same time.

When Ayden and I got to Karen's house, one of her stylist friends was over, too, and they had books of hair models spread out in front of them. Ayden was given tea-making duties, and Karen decided to get right into looking at my hair.

After making us amazing cups of Earl Grey with milk and honey, Ayden left to go to the doctor's to pick up a prescription. By this point I had an overall on and foils and dye in my hair. I had put on some music and was just letting Karen listen to my latest favourite track when Ayden came running back in, saying, 'Mum, can you come here for a minute?'

'What's wrong?' Karen blurted out.

'A cat's been run over out here and I don't know what to do!'

'*Kyle!*' Karen shouted, and I began heading for the door.

Looking up the road, I could see a guy standing there holding a large cat in his hands. Internally, I said, 'Thank you, angels and Archangel Ariel, for showing me what to do!'

'Don't worry – this won't bother me', I said to Karen as I ran towards the man.

The cat was lying facing upwards in his arms, wriggling with discomfort. She was a grey tabby with black markings and green eyes.

The man looked at me and said, 'I don't know what to do. I feel so bad.'

'Don't worry', I said. 'Pass her to me. I'm going to pray now.'

Ayden, Karen and her friend were all standing around me as I took the cat and placed a hand on her head.

'Thank you, angels and Archangel Azrael, for lovingly guiding this cat to heaven,' I said quietly. 'It's time for her to return home!'

Almost instantly the cat stopped wriggling. She had crossed over.

'She's in heaven now, guys – it's okay!'

Ayden began to fill up. She's a beautifully sensitive soul, so I instructed her to go to the doctor's and leave the rest to us. I also told the guy not to feel guilty. It was just one of those things.

I asked Karen to get me an old towel so we could wrap up the kitty and give her her dignity.

Neighbours gathered around, wondering what was going on, as I wrapped up the beautiful creature. I called the SSPCA for some advice on how we could give her a positive send-off and was told that the council could pick her up if she didn't have an owner. It turned out that she was a stray who was being fed by a neighbour. Another neighbour offered to bury her in the field next to her home alongside her other pets, and we agreed that was for the best.

Karen's friend said to me, 'You know, you turned a whole situation around there with what you did. It was actually quite emotional. It was as if this wave of serenity just washed over us all!'

As we made our way back inside, I looked up to see the most amazing rainbow arching over us. I took this as a sign that the little one had crossed the bridge safely to heaven.

Working with the Law of Grace

As well as sending healing prayers to a person or situation under the Law of Grace, you can also send positive thoughts out to people. Every time I see an ambulance, police car or fire engine drive past with its blue light on I say something like: 'Thank you, angels and anyone else who can help, for sending light and healing to this situation and all involved under the Law of Grace.'

You could also send prayers of grace out for:

- An animal rights or conservation campaign

- A developing country

- A charity campaign

- A friend or family member who needs a boost, or even just to be reminded that angels are there to help

- Anyone you feel could benefit from some positive energy

- A past event that still needs some healing.

~ 8 ~

ALIGNING PRAYERS
WITH LOVE

'Miracles occur as natural
expressions of love.'

A Course in Miracles

Everything in the universe carries a vibration, including
us, and our vibration can affect our spiritual connection
and the effectiveness of our prayers. If we're in a state
of fear, we create a wall around ourselves and our voice
isn't heard. If we're in a state of love, we lift ourselves
to heaven and our prayers are magnified.

I've found that when I'm in a calm and centred
place, my readings and spiritual communications work
far better. Of course they work when things aren't
100 per cent, but when I'm focused, it's as if I have a
broadband connection rather than dial-up.

Here are some easy ways to infuse your prayers
with love.

Release All Grievances

When we're holding grudges and grievances, especially concerning something we're praying about, there's a good chance that those grievances are blocking the angels from creating the answers we're seeking.

Resentment is like a barricade that keeps us shut out in fear and separation. It makes us feel cut off from our guardian angel and, ultimately, God. When we forgive, on the other hand, we reconnect with our true spiritual essence and align our soul with love.

A Course in Miracles says: 'Forgiveness lifts the darkness, reasserts your will and lets you look upon a world of light!'

(See Archangels Jeremiel and Zadkiel, pages 117 and 189, for support on forgiveness and mercy.)

Surround Yourself in Golden Light

As angels are beings of light, we can draw their energy to us by imagining ourselves being covered from head to toe in golden light. Gold is the colour of spiritual knowledge and wisdom. When we visualize it around us, we ignite our spirit, reach into the depths of our spiritual knowledge and open ourselves up to miracles.

Here's what to do:

© Sit with your spine erect and both feet on the ground, hip-width apart.

- ◎ Allow your hands to rest on your lap, palms facing upwards.

- ◎ Close your eyes, take three deep breaths into your solar plexus and as you breathe out think, *Relax, relax, relax...*

- ◎ Visualize a beautiful golden being standing behind you.

- ◎ See its feathered wings encircling you as protection.

- ◎ Imagine this golden being pouring a golden light over your body from top to toe.

- ◎ Allow the light to extend to every part of your body. See it flowing through your blood.

- ◎ Focus on your prayers in the affirmative angel prayer format.

- ◎ Say your prayers.

- ◎ When you've finished, thank the angels and open your eyes.

Do a Victory Dance!

This is something my friend David Hamilton taught me. At a workshop in Glasgow he explained that when we want to manifest things, it's good to act as though they've already happened. Personally, he does a victory dance!

I loved the concept and began doing it. When I wanted to write this book, I thanked the angels for supporting me, and visualized myself holding the finished book in my hands saying, 'Thank you, thank you, thank you!' and then I began dancing, raving and moonwalking around my office as if I'd just heard the best news in the world, while singing 'This Is How We Do It' by Montell Jordan over and over! Looking into the massive mirror hanging on the wall, I just couldn't help laughing at myself.

Not two minutes after I'd calmed down, my phone started ringing. It was my agent, calling to ask me to prepare for my next book! I was absolutely astonished by how quickly this had happened. I said, 'Clare, this is a miracle!'

It got even better when I opened my emails and found confirmation of a booking to go on live TV and speak about my work with angels!

I bet you're wondering how to do a victory dance now, aren't you?

© Say your prayers and acknowledge that what you want has already happened.

© Feel the excitement and rush of those amazing blessings.

© Maybe yell out 'Woo hoo!' or make some other sound that represents achievement to you.

© Thank the angels!

© Raise your arms and wiggle from side to side.

© Give it your best signature dance move and feel ecstatic!

Now I always victory dance as I'm focusing my intentions. I also victory dance when something goes right, and when I achieve something. It feels great. Victory dance your way to answered prayers!

Think a Safety Thought

It's very important to have a thought that you can focus on to make you feel safe and strong. When your ego kicks in and wants you to fear the worst, it can be so difficult to take your mind off it. For this reason I decided to come up with a safety thought that helped me really focus on beauty.

My safety thought has been the same for the past few years now: it's a sunflower. What I do is imagine a radiant sunflower glowing in the sunshine. Sometimes I begin to paint one mentally, a petal at a time, and then the beautiful brown centre, often with a smiley face on it to keep myself focused on joy. By the time I've added a beautiful tall green stem and a big red pot, I've brought myself back to a centre of calm.

I once shared my love of sunflowers with an audience, and just before Christmas last year one of the students left a beautiful book containing sunflower quotes and pictures on my doorstep. I look at it often.

When I've worked with clients on safety thoughts, some of them have been really creative. One person visualized himself as a deep-sea diver, swimming gently through the ocean with the most beautiful tropical fish and dolphins circling him. Others have imagined themselves as little kids laughing and playing on the beach, or even focused on their own children, either by looking at their photos or remembering the love and joy of seeing them for the first time.

Tips for creating a safety thought:

◎ Make it something you'll never forget! Something that makes you feel connected to life and love is best.

◎ Ensure it's something you can spend time going over or creating in your mind.

◎ Include bright and joyful colours that lift the spirit.

◎ Smile from ear to ear as you think about it.

◎ If you have trouble visualizing, carry a pocket-sized picture of your positive safety thought.

You can use your safety thought any time you need to feel strong and secure, and even when you are feeling aligned, as it will help to keep you positive.

Light a Candle

In the Catholic tradition, it's very common to light a candle for someone or in support of your prayers. It's also very popular in the Wiccan/pagan belief systems. Angels love candles because they burn so brightly.

When I light a candle, I always try and think about something positive because the flame is going to carry that intention for me. Even saying something as simple as 'Thank you, angels, for the blessings in my life' as you light a candle can really encourage more blessings to come to you.

I particularly like to light a candle when praying for others, because I want the light within it to shine on their lives and direct them to a place where their problems are solved.

(*See the Divine Mother Mary, page 197, for lighting candles for peace.*)

PART II

ANGEL DIRECTORY

～ THE ANGELIC HIERARCHY ～

Angels are multi-dimensional beings. Their energy and unconditional love is so vast that they can be many places at once, with no limitations.

There is a huge hierarchy of angels, made up of three tiers, called spheres. Each tier contains three groups, known as choirs.

The First Sphere
The first sphere is composed of angels known as the heavenly counsellors.

Seraphim
The Seraphim form the highest order of the angelic realm. They are so closely connected to the universal life-force that they ensure that all of the energy stemming from it is going where it is intended.

Seraphim means 'the burning ones', and these angels are flames of universal love. They are said to have six wings. They are known for their heavenly voices, and miraculous planetary shifts are reported to take place when they sing. Many texts say they are constantly singing the praises of God.

Cherubim

Cherubim means 'fullness of knowledge', and these beings are God's record-keepers. They are closely connected with the Akashic records – a chronicle of every event that has ever happened in the cosmos.

The Cherubim are said to direct the divine will of the universe and to have four faces and four wings so that they can look and fly in all directions.

Thrones

The Thrones are charged with carrying out the shifts of consciousness in the universe. Archangels Metatron and Sandalphon (*pages 129 and 177*) have close connections to this choir, as shown by the 'on' in their names.

The word 'Throne' relates to the seat of God, and it is said that these beings work through the web of life itself. They have been seen as wheels of light.

The Second Sphere

The angels of this sphere are said to be the universal governors.

Dominions

Dominions means 'lordships', and these powerful beings have a real sense of presence and authority. They regulate the roles of every other angel, except for those of the first sphere, and are seen holding orbs or sceptres to represent their authority. They also look after nations and international situations.

Virtues

The Virtues are the angels who oversee the movements of nature. Their name means 'strongholds', and they bestow blessings upon individual countries.

Powers

The Powers are the angelic choir who constantly send us reminders that there are better ways than war or destruction. These beings channel grace and mercy, encouraging all of us to be compassionate to the planet and, of course, one another.

The Powers can protect us from negative energy, and if called to a situation with low energy, they can dispel it instantly because their eyes burn with the love of the divine.

The Third Sphere

These are the messenger angels, the guardians and warriors who protect the planet and the people who call on them.

Principalities

The Principalities, whose name means 'rulers', are the protectors of spirituality and spiritual texts. These divine beings provide us with strength when things get tough. They have a strong connection with world leaders and with activists, particularly those who want to make truly compassionate changes to our planet. They encourage our inner leader, support our inner strength and inspire us to find peace.

They are also said to inspire new ideas in art and science, especially the science of physics, which helps us to understand our world more and more.

Archangels

Archangels are the best-known choir of angels because they are mentioned in Abrahamic texts such as the Torah, the Bible and the Koran. They are the 'boss angels' who watch over the guardian angels.

Archangels are always seen as huge beings – tall, full of life and carrying a tool or symbol of their spiritual purpose. For example, Archangel Michael is often seen carrying a flaming sword as a symbol of his ability to cut the cords that bind us to the past.

In the following chapters, I'll be looking at each of the major archangels in more detail.

Angels

This choir of angels includes the guardian angels who look after us and our daily needs. These are the beings we are praying to when we simply say 'Thank you, angels...'

These angels are probably the most human-like in appearance – they take on our looks so that we can understand them more easily. They were made to work hand in hand with us.

⁓ ARCHANGEL ARIEL ⁓

Ariel means 'Lioness of God', and Archangel Ariel is a powerful angel of courage and strength. When you connect with her energy, you should instantly feel uplifted and strong.

When I clairvoyantly connect to Ariel, I see her as a tall black African woman. She has a strong neck and shoulders, and her eyes are fiery red and orange. She has the most divine golden aura – it's as comforting as a warm fire in winter.

Ariel may be strong, a warrior angel, but she's graceful, too. When she enters a room, she lights everyone up from the inside out.

Ariel is a great angel to connect to when you need to stand your ground and be assertive without losing your temper. Many people think that being assertive is 'unspiritual', but if you continually get drawn into the negative side of situations, or say 'yes' when really you mean 'no', then you're giving away your power. Sometimes you do have to stand your ground.

This is Ariel's message to you:

'It is safe for you to be powerful and to use your voice. Being clear about what you will accept in your life and what you won't is a very liberating process. When you allow someone to have a hold over you, you give them your power. I come to you in love and with a nudge of support, encouraging you to take control. When you know you're safe, you absolutely are!'

The Angel of Animals

Ariel is the angel of animals and has a particular bond with those who are wild or homeless. She is brilliant with domestic animals, too, and can help us when it comes to lost pets, pets we can't understand and pets who are unruly or afraid. When called upon, she can bring great healing to animals. She is always around animal welfare activists, too, and is the voice that animals sometimes don't have.

I was asked by Ariel to remind you that pets and other animals feel loss, too, particularly when they have lived with a person or another animal for a long time and have experienced them making the transition to heaven. When you know of an animal going through something like this, call on Ariel for help, because it can be very traumatic for them, especially because they can't tell you how they're feeling.

When you're helping an animal through a difficult time, you can say affirmations for them and of course pray for support for them.

One of the things I do when I come into contact with animals that need some TLC, or just a pick-me-up, is put my hands on them if I can and say, 'You are loved, you are safe, you are well!' You can do this, too. As you do so, imagine the most amazing golden light flowing from heaven into these animals and know that this light will support them on their journey back to wellness.

Animal Guides

Many of us have an animal guide or guides who bring us support and messages. If you, like me, have that close bond with animals, work with Ariel, as she will open the doorway to the animal kingdom for you and help you to connect to your animal guide. I must say, though, that when you do this, do be prepared to support, help and guide animals at random times in your daily life.

Meditation for Connecting with Your Animal Guide

✧ Take a few slow deep breaths, breathing out a lot more than you breathe in.

✧ Imagine yourself being enveloped in a golden light from head to toe. Feel angels of light surrounding you.

✧ Say, 'Thank you, Archangel Ariel and animal guides, for coming close to me and for reminding me of your presence today! I am ready to connect to you!'

✧ Close your eyes and go on an inner journey to a favourite place such as a beach, forest or castle. When you arrive, your animal guide will be waiting for you, along with your vision of Ariel.

✧ Ask your guide questions, thank it for showing you the way and connect with its essence. It will have so much to offer you.

✧ When you feel you have received the answers to your questions and have interacted with your animal guides, thank them for being with you and for serving their purpose. Retrace your steps one by one until you find yourself comfortably back in the physical world. Wriggle your fingers and toes and open your eyes!

✧ It's always great to have some water and something sweet to ground yourself after meditation work.

Here are a few of the guides you might encounter, and their meanings:

Bear: The bear represents taking a step back. You are to retreat with your thoughts and concerns. Just like a bear, go into your cave, your safe place, such as your home, and relax.

Cat: The spirit of the cat brings so much. Cats lie around for hours thinking things through before they make a move, so if a cat is your guide, you're being encouraged to really assess the pros and cons of your situation before taking action. Your intuition will guide you.

Dog: The dog is the symbol of trust. As 'man's best friend', the spirit of the dog helps you discern who is trustworthy and shows up when it's safe for you to trust.

Dolphin: Dolphins bring freedom and joy. Have fun, don't be too serious and make the most of all of your experiences right now. If something is holding you back, release it!

Elephant: The elephant is a family guide. Elephants are selfless and strong and hold things together very well. When an elephant comes to you, you're being encouraged to connect to your family – they are your support.

Fox: A master of plans and disguise, the fox can think on his feet and deal with situations quickly and safely. When a fox comes to you, he shows an obstacle being overcome.

Hare: The hare represents the dreamer spirit. Your dreams, whether day or night dreams, are powerful connections to your higher self and to your future.

Lion: When a lion comes to you, you're being encouraged to stand your ground. Allow yourself to be strong like the lion, but remember to keep your cool as well.

Owl: If you see an owl, you must connect to your inner wisdom and listen to what you already know. When you deny the truth, your ego is in control. Connect with your truth and allow the divine to direct you.

Snake: This is a time for change! Snakes shed their skin every year to reveal a beautiful new silky body. When the serpent spirit comes to you, it's time to shed your old skin!

Tiger: You can't blend in, it's time to be yourself! The tiger brings you the medicine to love and accept yourself. Begin to see any 'flaws' as traits that make you unique. You are very much loved in heaven!

Turtle: The turtle is the guide who tells you to slow down, take your time and enjoy the journey. You may be impatient, but it's important for you to relax. Breathe!

Whale: Whale and orca energy is strong, vast and powerful. You are being given extra support to shine right now. You have so much to share, so you must believe in yourself.

Wolf: The wolf is an instinctive animal who works well in a pack. You have drawn this guide to you because you're being encouraged to trust your perceptions and your instinct. You already know what to do.

Connect with Ariel

Ariel can help us with any issues regarding animals and animal welfare, including lost pets, finding an animal to adopt or help, healing animals and helping an animal settle into a new home.

A Prayer to Ariel

Here's a prayer to welcome Ariel's energy into your life:

'Ariel, Lioness of God,

Thank you for surrounding me in your golden light.

I welcome your strength and assertiveness.

I feel warm and safe knowing you are with me now.

Thank you for unlocking my courage and helping me to see clearly.

Surround me with your animal guides.

I am free like the birds in the sky, like the lions in the wild.

Today I soar high, unchained, assertive and at peace.

Thank you, Ariel. I am the light, as are you. I am ready to shine!'

Ariel and Other Archangels

© Ariel and Azrael support animals when they are ready to cross over.

© Ariel, Gabriel and Haniel are what I'd call soul sisters — three powerful female archangels who will help groups of women get along and grow together.

© Ariel and Michael provide us with the strength to be assertive and feel safe.

© Ariel works with Raphael to bring healing to the animal kingdom.

∽ ARCHANGEL AZRAEL ∾

Azrael in Hebrew means 'God is my aid', and in Arabic 'He who helps God.' Azrael is the archangel of transition. He supports souls who are making their way to the other side. Whether they be human or animal, Azrael is the light that guides them through the tunnel to God.

When you Google Azrael, you will most likely find something like 'the angel of death' and images of a Gothic and frightening hooded figure. I have to say that Azrael is anything but that! He is a tall, handsome angel; and his energy is one of the most heartwarming, divinely beautiful energies you'll ever encounter. I always see him with dark skin, a chiselled chin and a purple, golden and red aura. I've seen him wear a cloak, but he does take his hood down when you ask him. He wears the cloak to hide himself, especially from the naked eye. I've always seen him as an angel who stays behind the scenes unless we consciously invite him in.

One of the most important energies that comes with Azrael is a sense of peace and comfort. He may be known as 'the angel of death', but he doesn't bring death, he supports us as we return home.

When his energy comes to us, it doesn't always represent a physical passing, but can also relate to moving from an old life to a new one. Azrael brings the energy of transition as we leave behind all that we no longer need, especially hurt and pain. He will gently guide us through a dramatic change in our life.

Azrael is non-invasive; he won't be overpowering. His energy is so gentle and light that we'll be eased through any transition.

He will also help us heal if we are in a great deal of pain due to losing a loved one or pet. Azrael is always there to support us at those times. His energy will surround us so that we'll feel closer to our loved ones than ever. He comes with the light of grace; he encourages us to find hope and strength.

Whenever Azrael comes through at the beginning of a session or reading, I know that I'm dealing with someone's grief and that they are struggling with it.

Azrael is also the angel who supports counsellors and others who work with those who have emotional troubles. He'll help us to find the right words without appearing interfering or invasive.

Whether you're a counsellor, a medium or someone who's dealing with grief, here's a message to you from Azrael:

'I create a bridge between heaven and Earth. It is my role to remind those on Earth that there is no separation between heaven and Earth. It is my aim that fear is taken from what you call "death", for it is nothing more than a transition of the soul. We angels massage the hearts of those who feel left behind because we want them to remember their divine origins. One day they will go home, too, but it is important to make the most of this earthly life.'

Another message that came through with Azrael was this:

'It's always okay! You may be dealing well with change or grief and then all of a sudden be dragged back into the pain. Allow yourself to breathe, allow yourself to remember — to remember love. Your loved ones are with you now — trust this. There's no rush to overcome loss. Take your time, allow us to guide you and know that you aren't on your own.'

Creating a Spirit Altar

A spirit altar is a sacred space dedicated to all our loved ones who have gone on before us. We can use it to honour them and to create a physical space to connect with them.

All you have to do is set aside a space somewhere in your house (facing east is probably best, as it relates to the element of air, i.e., spirit) and place items there that remind you of your loved ones, along with fresh flowers, crystals, candles – whatever you choose to make this a special place. Many people write notes, prayers and letters to their loved ones in heaven. Allow this space to be your 'spiritual postbox'.

You might like to say the following prayer:

'As I connect with this space, I create a bridge between heaven and Earth.

Thank you, Archangel Azrael, for reminding me there's no separation and for bringing the love of [name loved one(s)] *to me here.*

And so it is!'

Reminders from Heaven

When our loved ones are close, we may receive signs and reminders from them. If we would like the comfort of a sign, all we have to do is say a prayer, then expect a sign to show up.

Here are some signs and their messages:

Butterfly: A great symbol of transformation. When loved ones send you a butterfly, they want you to know they are free of pain, suffering and worry. They are settled in heaven; they have found peace.

Dragonfly: Seeing a dragonfly in an unusual place is a sign that a loved one in heaven is taking you on a journey. On the way, you'll learn so much about yourself that your heart will become complete again.

Music: Hearing music in your dreams, at unusual times or when you've been feeling down, is a sign of celebration. Your loved ones and angels want you to remember the joy and blessings in your life. As you focus on those blessings, the angels will guide you to happiness again.

Orbs and apparitions: When you see an orb or an apparition in a photo, angels and the spirit world are reminding you of their presence. Be conscious that angels and spirits are around you and are guiding you.

Rainbow: When connecting with Azrael, you may receive the sign of a rainbow. This can be sent in many forms – in the sky, on stationery or even in a song. It represents the promise that your loved ones will never leave your side.

Robin redbreast: The robin redbreast brings a message of hope. It's an encouraging sign to say that your loved ones are helping you deal with what's going on. It says that you are stronger than you realize and it's okay to talk to them – they can hear you.

Connect with Azrael

Azrael can help us with crossing over, bereavement and grief, leaving an old life behind as we move into a new one, losing the fear of death, finding the right words to say in emotional support and connecting to the other side.

Prayers to Azrael

Here's a prayer to welcome Azrael's energy into your life:

> *'Azrael, divine worker of God,*
> *Thank you for supporting me at this time.*
> *With your energy I create a rainbow bridge between heaven and Earth.*
> *I remember that there is no separation.*
> *God is here, present with me now.*
> *My loved ones are here, present with me now.*
> *I am never alone; I am always safe.*
> *I allow the light of heaven to guide me from fear to love.*
> *I undertake transitions safely on my journey. Thank you for supporting me!*
> *And so it is!'*

Use the following prayer to support a loved one who is either ready to cross over or has just crossed over. There is something really comforting about helping someone move to heaven. Send them angels, support and love.

> 'Archangel Azrael,
>
> Thank you for lovingly guiding [name of person] safely to heaven. I hand them to you and God, knowing you will do the best for them and for this whole situation.
>
> Thank you for comforting this person during this safe, gentle and natural transition to their rightful home!
>
> And so it is!'

Azrael and Other Archangels

- Azrael works with Ariel to help animals cross over.

- Azrael, Michael and Zadkiel are a powerful combination for transmuting and removing fear from a space or home.

✎ ARCHANGEL CHAMUEL ✎

Chamuel is the archangel of love and purpose. His name means 'He who sees God', and he is one of the seven major archangels. He is a tall, handsome angel with light blonde hair and a ruby aura. His eyes are piercing blue.

When I began to work with Chamuel, I was aware that he came straight to my heart. When we welcome his energy, he helps us open our heart so that we can receive the love and support we deserve. He knows that we all just want to be happy.

One of his most important roles is to help us move from our ego into our heart. A lot of the time we seek happiness outside ourselves — in our career, relationships, material possessions and so on. Chamuel is here to help us discover that the happiness we seek is within.

'He who sees God' also helps us to see the divine inside ourselves. If we accept this and constantly remind ourselves of it, everything in the outside world will reflect it back to us.

Chamuel's message:

'Your life is a reflection of how you view yourself. Everything external to you is indeed connected to you. However, if you seek happiness outside yourself, you'll lose your sense of rhythm and purpose. I am here to support you on your journey to love. This may not feel like an easy journey, but it is what you chose. Work with me and remember who you really are. Love circulates through your whole body and is coming straight from your true heart: your soul!'

Finding Our Purpose

Chamuel helps restore our sense of purpose. Most of us like to know what our role is – what we are supposed to do, who we are supposed to be. Our ego will tell us that our purpose is to be this, that and the next thing. It will also tell us that we have to make a certain amount of money, that we need to rush and that we're running out of time. What can we do?

Trust divine timing, focus within and, most important, remember to breathe. There's no pressure to find your purpose. You are a being of divine origin, and if you continually focus on this and surrender to heaven, God will direct you.

Instead of asking, 'What's my purpose?' ask, 'How can I serve today?'

By serving and supporting others, remembering your divine origins, focusing on love and allowing God's will to direct you, you are living your purpose!

Soul Mates and Twin Flames

Another important part of life is finding someone to share it with. Many people with spiritual mindsets aren't fulfilled in this sector of their lives and wonder why. It all goes back to Chamuel's message above: 'Your life is a reflection of how you view yourself.' I always feel that it is our recognition that we deserve a relationship that will create one. Remembering the love within us and focusing on it will allow others to see it, too.

Thinking about this, I began to wonder what the difference was between a soul mate and a twin flame, so I asked the angels for an answer. This was it:

'You can have more than one soul mate in a lifetime, but a twin flame is a soul who spends many lifetimes with you. These are the souls who help you feel complete, connected and strong. A twin flame is a soul who will reflect

*to you 100 per cent the love you have for
them and, of course, yourself. It is important
to say that a twin flame doesn't always have
to be a lover. It can be a child who comes to
remind you what love is, or it can be a parent
who is completely supportive of you.'*

Soul Mates in Heaven

If you feel you've had a perfect relationship but your
partner has gone to heaven, don't worry – this person
is still with you. When our soul mates go to heaven,
it becomes their duty to support us and love us
unconditionally. They will be there for us and in many
cases will send us another partner who will bring us
great happiness, often one who is very similar to them.

Angels want you to know that if you've lost a
spouse and feel guilty for moving on with a new
partner, it won't be held against you. It was probably
divinely guided. Your partner in heaven approves, and
loves and supports you. Please know they want you to
be happy.

Feng Shui for Love

In *feng shui*, the oriental art of placement, the far
right-hand corner of your home when you come in the
front door is linked to your love life and relationships.

When I've been to bless the home of someone who isn't fulfilled in love, I've usually found dust and clutter in this section of the house. If you're looking to improve your love life, assess this part of your living space. Does it have anything that represents love at all? Clear this space out, dust it, make sure it looks clean and place an item there that reminds you of love — perhaps a photo of your parents' wedding, a rose quartz crystal, a romantic picture such as 'The Kiss' by Gustav Klimt, or red or pink roses.

See Only Love

Chamuel encourages us to see only love in our lives. So many of us are drawn to the negative side of situations, myself included. But when we begin to work with Chamuel, he will help us see love in every situation.

If someone is acting insanely towards us, it's our job to reflect how we would like to be treated. Most of us are angry in a situation like this, continually relive it in our minds and even grind our teeth! But remember the Law of Attraction! We're bringing everything we think about into our life. So, if we want to begin changing a situation, we need to release it completely, bless it with love and let it go.

Sending Love to a Situation

Sending love to a situation is really simple and works wonders. All you have to do is think of the situation and imagine it surrounded by a light that reminds you of love. (I always imagine the whole situation and everyone involved, even the building, surrounded by a bright ruby-pink light.) Then say:

> *'Thank you, Archangel Chamuel and angels, for holding this situation, anyone involved and myself in a space of love.*
>
> *I surrender it to you and God, knowing you will do the best for everyone's highest good!*
>
> *And so it is!'*

You may need to do this more than once, but keep it up and you can change a fearful situation into a loving one.

Chamuel also 'sees God', and if 'God' means 'love', that means he sees love in everyone. He can help us to do this, too, and to move away from judgement and criticism. If we're drawn into criticizing others, all we're doing is sending out a wave of judgemental energy. And if you know anything about the sea, you'll know the tide always comes back in!

A Course in Miracles says: 'Exempt no one from your love or you will be hiding from a dark place in your mind', and it's absolutely true. By withholding your love from others, by not forgiving them or having negative thoughts about them or not accepting them, you're allowing your ego to run the show. And by 'hiding from a dark place in your mind', you're not allowing the light in and are creating a barrier between yourself and God.

The *Course* goes on to say: 'By not offering total love you will not be healed completely', and what it's saying here is that you're not holding anyone back but yourself. When we exempt others from our love and acceptance, we're holding ourselves back from being healed. Being healed means having no fear, no ego and living a life of love where everything is abundant. So, work with Chamuel to see the best in others with this short prayer:

> *'Thank you, Chamuel, for encouraging me to see the divine in myself and others.*
>
> *As I recognize the divine in everyone, a wave of love washes over my life that creates blessings and abundance.*
>
> *And so it is!'*

Connect with Chamuel

Chamuel can help us with finding our life purpose, finding a soul-mate relationship, sending love to a situation and seeing love in others.

A Prayer to Chamuel

Here's a prayer to welcome Chamuel's energy into your life:

> 'Loving Chamuel,
>
> *Thank you for surrounding my life with your ruby aura so that I can remember the most important lesson: that only love is real.*
>
> *It feels so good knowing I'm opening up my heart to receive the love and blessings I know I deserve. By connecting with your essence, I begin to see the divine in myself and in everyone around me.*
>
> *I now create a wave of love and good intentions that I send out into the world under the Law of Grace. I know this wave will return to its sender tenfold, so I continue to bless others and myself.*
>
> *Thank you, Chamuel, for perceiving the love inside me. I now open my eyes and see it clearly myself!*
>
> *And so it is!'*

Chamuel and Other Archangels

© Chamuel works with Michael to help us discern if our partner is being truthful.

© Chamuel and Raguel bring harmony and peace to a conflict.

- Chamuel works with Raphael to help us see love in a situation.

- Chamuel and Sandalphon can help us intuitively find our soul mate on Earth.

- Chamuel and Uriel help us in our career and business.

～ ARCHANGEL GABRIEL ～

Gabriel is the ultimate nurturing angel. She is a beautiful, curvaceous angel who has a really caring nature. She is described in the Bible and the Koran as male, but I've always seen her as female. In fact, as the angel of mothers, it makes complete sense that she'll appear as female. When you look at angel artwork, especially older work, you'll see that Gabriel's gender is always hard to define.

When I see her, she looks similar to the famous pop singer Adele. She has beautiful deep blue eyes, a heart-shaped face, and auburn hair that wraps around her. Her wings are pure pearlescent white. Although it is said that she is the keeper of the white ray, I always see pink and yellow sparkles around her. The white ray is a spiritual symbol of purification and grace. It is something we can consciously bring into our energy for purification and balance. You may have connected with this ray if you've visualized yourself being covered in a pure white light. In my eyes, the white ray helps us connect with the most divine part of ourselves: our soul. It helps us act from the heart, with integrity.

Gabriel's name means 'Strength of God', and she is said to be the archangel who visited the Divine Mother Mary to give her the news that Jesus was on his way. Gabriel, or Jibra'il, as she's known in Islam, is also said to have channelled the Koran to the prophet Mohammed. She is the bringer of good news, so every time she appears in a reading I know that good things are about to happen.

It is said that she plays a trumpet, and when it is blown, the doors to heaven open. I always see this as a metaphor for creating heaven on Earth. One of the most amazing things about working with angels is that they help us create a divine life filled with blessings. When we welcome Gabriel, she brings a host of good energy and celebration into our life.

As Gabriel is the bringer of good news, she's also very closely connected with communication. When we call on her, her energy will wrap around us, allowing us to feel safe so we can communicate our truth.

Recently I was interviewed live on a television show with over a million viewers, and although I was really excited, I knew I needed Gabriel's help to ensure my message was conveyed properly. I welcomed her into my aura via prayer and affirmation, and the interview couldn't have gone better.

Later that day, while enjoying a chilled soda water, I looked up to see the building I was sitting outside had 'Gabriel's Wharf' written on it. Gabriel had sent me a sign to say she was present!

After that interview, my first book shot to number three on the Amazon chart, the phone was red-hot with calls and my email exploded with enquiries. With Gabriel's help, I was shining my light!

Here's a message from Gabriel:

> *'By speaking your truth, you are sharing your light and aligning yourself with the presence of God. When you lock in your concerns, fears and setbacks, you are clogging up the spiritual centres that allow light to move through you. Welcome me and the angels I work with to boost your strength and your ability to speak up without fear!*

The Inner Child

As the angel of mothers, Gabriel looks after our inner child, too. The inner child is the big kid in each and every one of us. So many of us forget about this child, though, or feel that we missed out on a lot in our childhood. If there are things from your childhood that you feel are holding you back, Gabriel can help you to heal them and move forward.

When I have done inner child work with clients, or on myself, I've always found it helpful to connect with the child via visualization. One of my favourites is the following:

- Imagine yourself as a child running through a field filled with daisies, or any other flower that reminds you of your childhood.

- As you run, see yourself having the best time — giggling, laughing and enjoying being free.

- Waiting in the distance is a tall female angel with auburn hair floating in the wind. You can see her full body and smell her sweet perfume.

- As you reach this angel, feel her embrace you. She wraps not only her arms but her whole energy around you. You feel safe in her bubble of light.

- Enjoy this loving, nurturing light before allowing it to extend to people from your childhood who bothered you, incidents that still haunt you or anything else that you feel has affected you. Don't be surprised if random events you thought you'd forgotten about come to mind — the angels will show you what you need to see.

© When you feel you've done all you need to at this time, thank Gabriel, go back through the field and open your eyes!

Here's a prayer to heal the inner child:

'Dear Archangel Gabriel,

Thank you for surrounding my inner child in your nurturing light and for helping it find peace.

I take this opportunity to tell my inner child that it is safe and loved and that nothing can come between it and the love it deserves.

As I nurture this divine and innocent part of myself, I heal my heart, I heal my soul, I open my mind and I'm able to see with new eyes.

I now reach out into the wonder of life, knowing Gabriel's light is guiding me.

And so it is!'

Conception

Gabriel can help with conception, too. She can work with you to ensure your body is healthy enough to create a baby. She protects women when they're pregnant and helps them to be strong if there are any setbacks.

Here's a prayer to assist with manifesting a baby. Remember that when you're focusing on creating something, you speak as if it has already happened. This allows you to really align your body with your prayers.

> *'Divine angels and Archangel Gabriel, thank you for surrounding me with your light and supporting me at this time.*
>
> *It's a joy to be a woman and bring life-force to this planet.*
>
> *I feel so blessed holding this bundle of joy in my arms!*
>
> *And so it is!'*

Connect with Gabriel

Gabriel can help us with creating good news, opening up and speaking our truth, healing any childhood issues and conceiving and supporting an unborn baby.

Prayer to Gabriel

Here's a prayer to welcome Gabriel's energy into your life:

> *'Archangel Gabriel,*
>
> *Strength of God, bearer of good news,*
>
> *Thank you for supporting me as I open up and speak my truth.*
>
> *I feel strong and empowered, knowing you are with me as I speak with integrity.*

*As you connect with me, I begin to see through
the eyes of my inner child.*

I begin to follow my joy and live with happiness.

I feel nurtured and know I am loved!

And so it is!'

Gabriel and Other Archangels

◎ Gabriel, Ariel and Haniel help groups of women get along and grow together.

◎ Gabriel works with the Divine Mother Mary, who can also help with children, conception and inner child issues.

◎ She can also work directly with Michael so that we can feel protected and speak our truth.

∽ ARCHANGEL HANIEL ∞

Archangel Haniel governs the moon and its spiritual connections. Her name means either 'Grace of God' or 'Glory of God', and she has an amazing pearly white and light blue aura.

Haniel reminds me of the pop singer Shakira. She has a shamanic priestess feel, with long golden locks that seem to move in the wind. Her skin is pearly white and her eyes are deep brown.

Haniel's energy helps us awaken our natural gifts and talents. She allows us to connect to the true spirit of grace and to see clearly where our life is taking us. She has a particular connection to women and sensitive people who are born with second sight.

People experience clairvoyance in different ways – seeing visions, auras or dreams; randomly seeing repeating numbers; seeing feathers or other symbols such as horseshoes or magpies, etc. Whatever way our clairvoyance works, Haniel can help us strengthen our connection.

When we work with Haniel and her divine luminance, we naturally open up our third eye. The third-eye chakra is located between the brows and governs our ability to perceive. If we're having problems with our physical or psychic sight, it could mean that this chakra is blocked or doesn't have enough energy. Haniel can help balance this.

Haniel's energy has a lunar effect – when she works with us, she can bring a tide of change that affects our whole life. As the glory of God, she enables us to see our divine gifts and qualities. She reminds us that these aren't always intense; they can be so subtle that we miss them. But when we call on this angel, she will illuminate them so that we can shine as a glorious child of God.

Here is a message from Haniel:

'It is your spiritual right to be strong and graceful; it is your spiritual right to see with great clarity. Within each soul who walks the Earth there lies the ability to connect with and exercise these great angelic qualities. If you work with me and my luminous light, I will support you in unleashing and expressing the divine from the inside out. Welcome me in – I am here to serve you!'

Goddess Connections

Because of the strong Goddess connections with the moon and the moon's links with the menstrual cycle, Haniel can support women through any menstrual issues or even menopause. If you have any concerns in these areas, call on her for support.

We all – even men – also have an inner goddess. This is the part of us that is strong and focused. It's the part Haniel can empower. She stands by us like a sister, friend and guide, encouraging us to see our qualities as a soul. When we connect to our inner goddess, we balance the receptive, psychic and feminine sides of our body and personality. Haniel can offer help in these areas now.

Full Moon Magic

Those of you who feel drawn to Earth-based spiritual traditions such as Wicca and paganism will love Haniel's energy. She is a high priestess who can help you connect with the moon and its magic.

Most types of magic and manifestations are best focused on at the time of the full moon, as this phase represents the 'mother' aspect and is when the moon's influence is at its most powerful.

You can really strengthen your connection to Haniel by meditating under the full moon or by visualizing full-moon energy washing over your whole body. See that blushed white luminous energy radiating around you.

As you do this, you are connecting to the divine within you, to tides of positive change and to the energy of grace.

The semi-precious gem moonstone has close connections with the moon and therefore Haniel's energy. If you place it on a window ledge during the full moon, you can call on Haniel to bless it. By carrying it with you in a bra (if you're female) or a sock (if you're male), you can draw in Haniel's divine qualities.

By placing your crystals, angel cards, tarot cards or any other healing tools on a window ledge at the time of the full moon, you can also ask Haniel to bless them and can ask the moon to charge them. This is likely to heighten your natural psychic and intuitive abilities.

Here's the prayer to say when you leave the tools to be charged:

'Archangel Haniel, thank you for your divine blessings on these tools.

I now leave them to be charged by your light and lunar magic, knowing they will have heightened support and connection to heaven.

And so it is!'

Connect with Haniel

Haniel can help us with focusing our gifts and talents, balancing menstrual cycles, opening our third eye, connecting with the moon, unleashing our inner goddess and performing divine magic.

A Prayer to Haniel

Here's a prayer to connect with Haniel's energy:

> *'Haniel, Goddess of the Moon and Angel of Grace,*
> *Thank you for shining your radiant light upon my life.*
> *I allow myself to open and connect with your spirit and poise.*
> *I connect with my inner wisdom, my inner vision.*
> *I open my eyes and see clearly with love.*
> *My gifts and talents naturally progress in your light,*
> *And the natural polarities within me are balanced.*
> *I stand with poise and in glory.*
> *I now create the life I deserve in your light and that of the creator.*
> *And so it is!'*

Haniel and Other Archangels

◎ Haniel, Ariel and Gabriel will help groups of women get along and grow together.

◎ Haniel can work with Raphael and Raziel to help us cultivate our spiritual gifts and clairvoyance.

◎ As Haniel governs the moon and Uriel the sun, they can work together to bring polarity and balance. I'd work with them both for jetlag and chemical imbalance issues such as Seasonal Affective Disorder (SAD) and bipolar disorder.

❧ ARCHANGEL JEREMIEL ❧

Jeremiel is a miracle worker. He is a brilliant archangel who helps us undertake an inventory of our life so that we can fix, remove or change anything that isn't serving us.

Jeremiel has a tall and slender body. He is a gentle angel but holds a torch representing illumination. His aura is bright orange and gold, the colours of passion and spiritual insight. He has shoulder-length golden hair and golden skin. His eyes are the deep blue of the night sky. He wears a cloak of wisdom.

Living a Life of Service and Mercy

Jeremiel is said to have given people tours of heaven. I feel that his presence helps us create heaven on Earth.

His name means 'God's mercy', and 'mercy' can mean a few different things. It can mean forgiving someone and being compassionate about a situation, but it can also mean living a life of service and being charitable towards others. So many of us are easily drawn into 'What do I want?' or 'What do I need?' whereas Jeremiel's energy helps us ask the question: 'How can I be of service?'

When we connect with Jeremiel, he will help us make the positive changes that we need in order to live a life of fulfilment.

I feel that Jeremiel always comes with a real sense of reassurance. He helps us find inner peace, especially if we've been through a lot of turbulence.

Here's the message I received from Jeremiel:

'You're always okay, because God has never left you. I want to reassure you that you can change your pathway. Reviewing your life is important because then you can allow yourself to be honest and focus on the life you are really here to live. If you are ready to forgive others, and ultimately yourself, and acknowledge any painful situations as illusions, you are free.'

What Jeremiel is saying here is very important: he's inviting us to turn our regrets and grievances into illusions. They arise from a state of fear, and only love is real. When we acknowledge this and forgive, we set ourselves free, and open our heart to the miracles of heaven.

Take some time to meditate on your life and say the following prayer:

'Thank you, Archangel Jeremiel, for helping me to recognize the illusions in my life as I prepare to set myself free!'

Then allow yourself to review some of the things in your life that you feel are holding you back. Are you hanging on to grievances or holding grudges? Go straight to the situation involved and say:

'You are not real.

You are an illusion.

Only love is real!'

Do this until you feel that you've let go of everything you no longer need and have made room for miracles and what I like to call 'the good stuff'.

The Miracle Mindset

The miracle mindset is when we expect miracles instead of dreading the future. One of Jeremiel's biggest messages is that if we allow our minds to meet God, then it is impossible for us to let fear in, so our lives will be free of setbacks and full of miracles.

Working with Jeremiel, we will become more aware of the actions that create illusions and disharmony in our lives and can learn to avoid them completely. If we feel ourselves slipping back into the old ways, we can just say this little affirmative prayer:

'Thank you, God and Jeremiel, for entering into my mind and highlighting the miracles in my life. It feels so good to live a life filled with mercy!

I am a light and I know I am loved!'

Connect with Jeremiel

Jeremiel can help us with reviewing our lives, living a life of service and mercy, recognizing the illusions that hold us back, forgiving others and having a miracle mindset.

A Prayer to Jeremiel

Here's a prayer to welcome Jeremiel's energy into your life:

'Jeremiel, Angel of Mercy, Server of the Light,

Thank you for entering my energy and awakening the miracles within.

I allow my illusions to be shown to me in visions and dreams.

As I acknowledge these illusions, I release them.

I remember the divine spark of love that is within me.

I acknowledge that this love connects me to all that is.

Forgiveness is a natural part of who I am.
I am free, I am merciful.
And so it is!'

Jeremiel and Other Archangels

◎ Jeremiel and Jophiel encourage us to have a positive mindset.

◎ Jeremiel works with Zadkiel on forgiveness and mercy.

✎ ARCHANGEL JOPHIEL ✎

Jophiel was the archangel who guarded the Tree of Life in the Garden of Eden. She is strongly associated with nature. Her name means 'God's beauty', and one of her main purposes in life is to help us see the beauty of the world around us.

I always see Jophiel looking similar to a Hawaiian woman. She has that gorgeous bronze skin and those deep chestnut-brown eyes, and her hair is long, dark and flowing. She moves very gracefully. Sometimes I see her carrying a star in her hand, and sometimes it sits on her forehead. She reminds me of the pop star Nicole Scherzinger, who is a Hawaiian goddess herself.

Jophiel is one of my favourite angels. She comes in like a breath of fresh air and encourages us to release monkey chatter from our mind and clutter from our home. If your home has a lot of tired, stuck energy in it, open all your windows and let the air in. If you feel that you're being tied down by work or that your creative flow is blocked, get outside and breathe deep fresh air into your lungs. Jophiel will help you! When I work in my office, I often welcome her in to clear the space so that the energy resonates with love.

What's great about Jophiel is that there's no messing around with her. She gets straight to work and has a real sense of assertiveness. She'll help us wake up and listen, she'll point out the clutter that's holding us back and she'll encourage us to slow down and appreciate the beauty in our lives right now.

This reminds me of when Maxine, a girl I know, said to me, 'It's not about where you're going, or where you've been, it's about – look at that view!'

That totally made sense. So many of us are too busy thinking about what's happening next on our schedule or remembering what has happened to us in the past to take in the beauty that's right in front of us. Jophiel helps us focus on the present moment. Here's a message from her:

> *'Pause for a second and take a deep*
> *breath. As you exhale, you are releasing*
> *old patterns from your mind and body.*
> *Work with me to beautify your inner self,*
> *to recognize your inner light and to build*
> *the confidence to share it. You may not feel*
> *adequately prepared for all of your future*

endeavours, but your divine self, your soul, that infinite spark within you that never ceases to be is prepared for everything. It is time, friend, to share your light with this planet. I will help you!'

Silencing the Voice of the Ego

Jophiel can really help us have confidence and silence the voice of doubt and fear – the voice of the ego – especially if we're about to do some spiritual work such as angel card readings, Reiki or meditation.

If you're one of those people who constantly doubts the spiritual information they receive, then Jophiel is your woman. She'll bring the confidence to allow you to trust. If you ask her, she'll also help you to distinguish between the voice of spirit and the voice of ego so that you can further your spiritual development.

Discovering Beauty Inside and Out!

Jophiel is the beauty of God, but beauty is within us, too. As we welcome Jophiel into our lives, she'll help us to be comfortable in our own skin and truly appreciate ourselves. Our body is our physical shell, and it's also the home of our mind while we're here. Jophiel's energy will declutter both body and mind so that we can dispel the barriers of fear and see the beauty in ourselves.

She will also help us to discover our soul's truth. As we connect with this truth, we'll align our whole life with love, with God and with our purpose. And nothing is more important than that.

One of the affirmations that Jophiel brings through is simple:

'I am the beauty of God!'

Say this affirmation at every available opportunity for two weeks and see how your life changes and how others view you.

Connect with Jophiel

Jophiel can help us with clearing clutter and old energy, silencing the voice of the ego, discovering our inner beauty and aligning our lives with love.

A Prayer to Jophiel

Here's a prayer to welcome Jophiel's energy into your life:

I breathe deeply and fill my core with fresh clean air.

As I exhale, I release the clutter of my mind and body.

Doing this, I allow myself to see and hear more clearly.

Thank you, Jophiel, for supporting me as I discover my inner beauty,

And for silencing the voice of my ego so that I can clearly hear God.

I feel so alive knowing your wings are taking me forward.

And so it is!'

Jophiel and Other Archangels

◎ Jophiel works with Jeremiel on encouraging us to have a positive mindset.

◎ Call on her and Raziel to deepen your awareness and still the mind in meditation.

∽ ARCHANGEL METATRON ∾

Archangel Metatron's name could possibly come from the Hebrew *Meta thronon*, 'the throne next to the divine'. This would automatically connect this archangel to the choir of Thrones in the angelic hierarchy.

Metatron is a special angel because he once walked the Earth as a human. He was known as Enoch and was a prophet and scribe who gained so much knowledge of the divine that when he came to pass away, he ascended to archangel status.

Metatron is a beautiful young angel. He's one of the tallest angels I've ever seen, but will also come in at an approachable height. He has light brown hair, bronze skin, deep indigo eyes and a really chiselled chin — think a darker-skinned Robert Pattinson from the *Twilight* movies. He wears magenta robes.

Metatron has a lot to do with our planet's changes and transitions. At the moment, he's helping us harness the new energies that are being offered to us by the universe. I call him 'the angel who connects heaven to Earth'. With his human experience and angelic knowledge, no one could do it better. One of the things I feel when I work with Metatron is that he helps me connect to Earth and heaven at the same time. It's as if he's showing us how to walk our talk!

The New Kids on the Block

As an ascended master, Metatron shows the way for the new kids on the block, the Earth angels, the future leaders and warrior spirits who are going to lead us to harmony. They are known as indigo, crystal and rainbow children – they're the future prophets, psychics and healers who are already here teaching and sharing their love.

Indigo Warriors

A huge influx of indigos arrived from the late 1980s to the late 1990s, although some did come much earlier. I call these amazing souls indigo 'warriors' rather than 'children', because most of them are adults now. They are natural-born psychics with fiery and rebellious spirits. I've been told many times that I'm one of them!

A lot of these souls chose families that needed to be reminded what love was, so they came to broken homes, to low and lost parents or were adopted. They are highly sensitive, hyperactive beings who can go from cool and collected to destructive in the flick of a switch. Many of them have been labelled with ADD, ADHD, autism or OCD. If they can remember their divine origins, however, they can become powerful psychics, leaders and peace entrepreneurs.

They can spot liars in an instant, and although they might be hot-headed, generally they have every reason to be! One of the greatest things about the indigo generation is that it has a passion for truth and integrity. Indigos will share this with you.

Sadly, many indigos have lost their way in life, but Metatron can help get them back on track. If you know someone with indigo qualities, send him to them now.

Crystal and Rainbow Children

Crystal and rainbow children are souls who seem older than their years or who have been here before. They are born with bright, passionate eyes and are so loving, kind-hearted and generous. They have natural compassion and will forgive easily. Generally they are born into safe environments and families because they need to concentrate on reaching out and touching as many people as possible. They can see people's auras and will do their best to heal their pain.

I have met some of these souls and just can't contain my emotions when I connect with them. Their hearts emanate a divine love that is very similar to that of the angels and ascended masters.

These kids are very sensitive, and many of them have been bullied at school, but they won't lose their temper; they'll just show love to the bullies. They'll forgive them and will seize every available opportunity to teach love.

Many of these kids will find themselves being drawn to religion and spirituality. Some of those I've met have loved going to church, singing hymns and saying their prayers. It's as if they're incarnated buddhas. They have such deep inner peace, and they want to show love and compassion for all life – so don't be surprised if you see them becoming vegetarian!

Metatron can help these kids on their soul missions. If you know kids like this, introduce them to this angel.

Here's a prayer to support all the new kids on the block:

'Metatron, Throne next to the divine,

Thank you for wrapping your crystalline energy around [name of soul] and for guiding them. I'm so grateful that they are fulfilled, have a sense of purpose and remember who they truly are.

We allow you in to show them how to shine their amazing light and discover their true leadership qualities!

And so it is!'

The Indigo Ray

Indigo warriors embody the energy of the indigo ray, which shines on our planet from the universe. We can connect with this energy in order to understand the indigos or even take on some of their super-sensory qualities.

The indigo ray is protected by Metatron and the indigo angels, who will respond to our request to connect. We can also visualize ourselves being immersed in an indigo light. This will enable us to awaken our inner psychic abilities and strengthen our assertiveness.

The Crystalline Ray

The crystalline ray is a step up from the indigo. It goes beyond the psychic and presents us with an inner knowingness. We can work with it, but to do so we have to practise forgiveness.

With the crystalline ray comes compassion — it washes through every cell of our body and helps us radiate light wherever we go. To clairvoyants and seers, our energy will look similar to the reflection of a sun-catcher sitting in a window.

Although Metatron's aura has close connections to deep magenta and indigo, he carries the crystalline ray, too.

Aligning the Chakras

Chakra is a Sanskrit word meaning 'wheel' and is used to describe a spiritual energy point on the body. There are seven main chakras running in a rainbow spectrum from the base of the spine to the top of the head. Each has both physical and non-physical connections:

- The root chakra, Muladhara, 'root support', is found at the base of the spine. It is red and is linked to our foundations, such as our home, family, finances and comfort zone.

- The sacral chakra, Svadisthana, 'one's own place', is found just below the navel. It is orange and is linked to our reproductive system and sexual organs.

- The solar plexus chakra, Manipura, 'place of jewels', is found in the stomach area. It is yellow and is linked to our willpower, drive and energy.

- The heart chakra, Anahata, 'unstuck', is found in the heart centre. It is green and is linked to our ability to love, share and practise altruism.

- The throat chakra, Vishuddha, 'pure place', is found in the throat area. It is blue and is linked to our communication skills and ability to speak with integrity.

© The third eye chakra, Ajna, 'command', is found between the brows. It is indigo, is linked to our perception and governs our ability to see clairvoyantly.

© The crown chakra, Sahasrara, 'lotus of 1,000 petals', is found at the top of the head. It is violet and linked to our spiritual connections and beliefs.

Chakras can have excessive energy or lack it completely. You can call on the angels to regulate them. Metatron and Raphael, in particular, will help bring them into balance.

The Soul Star Chakra

There is also a soul star chakra located six inches above our crown. This is our connection to divine guidance. When we connect to this six-pointed geometric shape, we align our chakras with the crystalline and indigo rays so that we have the ability to lead and be assertive but also have compassion and love for others. When we really align with this star, through meditation and prayer, we bring about great shifts in our body-mind-spirit connection. Call on Metatron to support you in aligning with your soul star chakra and connecting with the divine guidance that heaven is offering you. I call this connection 'checking in with heaven':

◎ Close your eyes and take several deep breaths through your nostrils. Feel yourself relaxing and becoming centred.

◎ Visualize a six-pointed star above your head shining a crystal-clear light over your whole body.

◎ Breathe in this divine light and feel your connection to heaven growing. As you do this, thank Metatron for his presence and for helping you to connect to the universal wisdom being offered.

◎ Ask about any situations on which you need light or advice.

◎ There's another great little thing you can say, too:

'Dear universe, thank you for directing me to what you would have me do, where you would have me go and what you would have me say.'

◎ Then just surrender into the meditation and go with the guidance offered, however that comes to you.

◎ When you feel ready, acknowledge your blessings and give thanks for all that you have received. Then open your eyes.

◎ Remember to write yourself some notes of wisdom!

In meditations or visualizations like this, I record myself on my phone talking myself through the steps and prayers so that during the meditation I can relax and not wonder if I'm 'doing it right'.

It's also important to say that this is all about intention and you can go on your own wee journey if you like! Trust that the angels will guide you.

Divine Timing

Archangel Metatron can also help us with any time issues or constraints. Since the turn of the millennium, you may have felt that time has sped up. So many lightworkers (those who have chosen to be here and live a life of love) find themselves running late nowadays and losing track of time. With his planetary knowledge, Metatron can help us adjust to these changes and get back on schedule.

Use this prayer or something similar:

'Thank you, Metatron, for adjusting time so that I'm back on schedule!
I ask all for the highest good and know that timing is always divine!'

Here's a message from Metatron:

'In heaven there are no limitations of time and space. When you work with me I will help you align and anchor your spiritual power to work efficiently and to recognize the priorities on your pathway. Within each man and woman

lies a warrior spirit who is waiting to lead the way. By anchoring your soul star and allowing yourself to shine like a crystal, you will step into your warrior spirit and will lovingly guide others to spiritual growth and help them see the love that is within!'

Connect with Metatron

Metatron can help us with settling indigo, rainbow and crystal children; realigning our chakras; connecting with divine guidance and getting back on schedule.

A Prayer to Metatron

Here's a prayer to welcome Metatron's energy into your life:

'Metatron, Archangel of Ascension,

Thank you for coming to me with your energy that goes beyond time and space.

As your magenta, indigo and crystalline rays surround my being, my soul adjusts to the here and now and I find purpose in the present and allow divine guidance to carry me forward.

My chakras align with love and I prepare to create heaven on Earth!

And so it is!'

Metatron and Other Archangels

© Metatron works with Orion and Sandalphon to help us adapt to the spiritual shifts that are taking place on the planet.

© Metatron and Raphael work together to clear our body and energy. They're also a great combination to call on if you're a Reiki practitioner.

© Metatron and Sandalphon work together to ensure we can have a spiritual connection without having to lose our balance as a 'human'.

❧ ARCHANGEL MICHAEL ❧

Archangel Michael, 'He who is like God', is probably the best known of all the angels. He is the archangel of protection and strength, and makes sure that the archangels and guardian angels carry out their duties.

Michael is one of the tallest angels there is. He has a beautiful cobalt blue aura, carries a sword of light or fire and is a great warrior who will support us as we overcome our fears. When I look into his eyes, I see fire and light swirling around in them. He connects us with the element of fire.

Each and every lightworker has Michael's energy. He protects us from lower energies and hostile thoughts. He wants to support us in being confident and knowing what is right.

The sword of light that Michael carries, also known as 'the sword of truth', is a powerful symbol. It removes the barriers of fear, the cords of the past and the chains that bind us to anger. With one quick swoop of his sword, Michael sets us free.

I learned about Archangel Michael when I was just 15 years old and began reading angel cards. He was the *only* archangel in my favourite deck, *Healing with the Angels Oracle Cards* by Doreen Virtue. This deck completely changed my life and my perceptions of who I was. Ten years on, I still use it and call on Michael every day.

Michael is the angel who really encourages us to trust the messages we're receiving and to serve others. So many of us have learned a lot of spiritual truths during the course of our lives but don't feel qualified to share them. If this is you, here's Michael's message to you:

> *'You are already qualified to share what you know about spirituality because you are spirit. There is a great light inside you that is desperate to shine, and I am here to help you. Call on me to dissolve the barriers and blocks that hold you back so that you are able to stand strong and share. By having faith in the higher power, you are invited to take the leap forward, spread your wings and allow them to carry you to new heights! It's the perfect time!'*

Allow this message to be your invitation to take the first steps, and then, by taking the next steps when they are presented to you, you will find God, life and angels paving the way ahead!

Cutting the Cords

Michael will come to all those who call on him to cut the cords that are holding them back. His sword is so powerful and strong that nothing can stop its force.

It's a good idea for us to cut the cords regularly. When we're around a negative experience or people unload their drama on us, the negative energy can hook on to our auras without our even noticing it. This doesn't make a *person* negative, by the way – it's just the energy that's created by a certain situation. If you've ever felt unrested or unexplainably angry, not been able to get to sleep or had nightmares, it's your body trying to process and release the negative energy. By working with Michael, you'll release it instantly.

You can cut the cords in two ways, either through prayer or visualization. I personally do both.

Visualization for Cutting the Cords

✧ Imagine yourself in a safe place filled with light, with angels all around you.

✧ Now imagine old situations, people's views of you and connections as ribbons of energy coming from your body.

✧ Once you feel you have cords all over your body, welcome Archangel Michael in to cut them. Imagine a tall, handsome angel coming with his sword of light and cutting these cords as easily as if he were taking a

pair of scissors to ribbons. See them cut through and
fall away.

✧ When you feel they have all been cut, thank the
angels and Michael and open your eyes.

This prayer may also help:

*'Thank you, Archangel Michael, for cutting the
cords that bind me to people, situations and old
energy.*

I am free.

*As I welcome your energy, I am filled with strength,
and your light of protection washes over me!*

And so it is!'

Dispelling Negative Energy

I clear out old energy regularly in my work and have
found that Archangel Michael can be invited in by
prayer to clear a home or space of its negative energy.
I really believe that negative energy and 'negative
spirits' are generally people's projections of fear
rather than anything else. I always encourage people
not to be afraid, because that's only going to create a
fearful situation.

Archangel Michael works very closely with Master
Jesus to bring healing and unconditional love to a space
that really needs it. Whenever I've felt uncomfortable

or been challenged by a situation, I've found that they're the ultimate combination of ascended masters to bring in.

Here's a prayer you could use:

'Heavenly hosts Archangel Michael and Master Jesus,

Thank you for being with me right now.

With your sword of truth, Michael, cut the cords of fear, the barriers of doubt and the chains of anger surrounding this situation. As you do so, see them transformed into love.

Thank you, Jesus, for blessing me with your sacred heart and for lovingly guiding me.

I forgive all that needs to be forgiven and become a light to the world with my purified heart. I surrender to the divine will, knowing that only good lies before me!'

Jesus has a heart of unconditional love and can be asked in by anyone, no matter what their beliefs or religious status. His energy isn't exclusive, it's universal. He's an open-hearted teacher who really changes the whole atmosphere. If you're ever in a place where you feel threatened and fearful, he's definitely the man to make you feel at ease.

I recently conducted a private session for a lady who was up against her ex-partner and his powerful family over the custody of their daughter. His family members were religious Nigerians who had taught the young girl curse words, and she continually called her mother 'the devil' in their native language.

When I tuned into the situation, I really felt oppressed. It looked as if the family had been trying to use some sort of 'mojo' on this lady. She admitted she'd wondered if she was being cursed or negative spirits were involved, and although I didn't see that, I knew I was beginning to get uptight about the situation and it was my job to remain neutral. I needed help.

I said to her, 'You're the keeper of your mind and body. But if you feel that this family has power over you, they will have power over you. I feel that this situation needs a great light in it, so I'm going to invite in Jesus and Archangel Michael.'

As soon as I closed my eyes and welcomed them in, the energy of my office changed completely. The energy around the woman began to transform, too, and she said that every hair on her body began to stand on end.

At this point I could see clearly what was going on. The man had been thinking about taking the girl on holiday and not coming back. When I told the lady, she said, 'Yes, he's been trying to take her out of the country for quite some time. I've always opposed the idea.'

Jesus and Michael cut the cords of fear that were around this woman and contributing to her challenges. Then they filled her heart with loving golden light.

Afterwards, she felt amazing. She picked her remaining angel cards and they clarified that the situation would now be resolved. I'll never forget that her final card was 'Miracles'. I tell you, one was certainly performed that day.

Connect with Michael

Michael can help us with overcoming fear, gathering strength, protecting our energy, cutting the cords that are holding us back and moving forward on our path.

As Michael's aura is blue, you can connect to him by imagining yourself completely surrounded in a cobalt blue light, or by using this colour in your clothing, bed sheets or even on your walls.

A great affirmation for this is:

'I am surrounded and enveloped in the blue light of protection by Archangel Michael!'

A Prayer to Michael

Here's a prayer to welcome Michael's energy into your life:

'Archangel Michael, Heavenly Host,

I am so grateful for your light and presence.

I welcome your energy into my life at this time.

I surrender and release all of the fears I no longer need.

I release all resistance, worries and concerns to heaven, knowing I am fully supported.

Thank you, Michael, for cutting the cords that bind me to people, places and situations.

The road ahead is clear. I recognize that I deserve freedom and accept it from this moment forward.

Only good lies before me and I am protected by your light. I am safe.

And so it is!'

Michael and Other Archangels

◎ Michael works with Ariel to provide us with the strength to be assertive and feel safe.

◎ Michael, Azrael and Zadkiel are a powerful combination for transmuting and removing fear from a space or home.

◎ Michael works with Chamuel to help us discern if our partner is being truthful.

◎ Michael and Zadkiel can help us overcome fears or phobias.

✥ ARCHANGEL ORION ✥

Orion's Belt is the planetary retreat of a *new* archangel who is now making his energy available to our planet. This archangel brings new information for a new world and helps us connect with the cosmos so that we can understand our special place in the universe.

Archangel Orion is a vast angel who appears as a handsome figure made up of stars, looking down upon us from above. His aura is like the night sky, with deep blues, indigos and glints of light shining through it.

Discovering Orion

How I learned about Orion is a story in itself. At the start of 2012, my angels kept telling me about a new archangel who was making himself known to the planet. I was really excited about this.

Then in June my publishers welcomed me to London for the launch of my first book and gave me some tickets to a workshop with Doreen Virtue. I was thrilled, because Doreen has been a great inspiration to me and, as I mentioned, I use her cards every day!

During one of Doreen's meditations, we were encouraged to ask our angels what we needed to know about 2012 and our own lives. In my head I just kept hearing 'Orion' over and over again. That night, lying in bed, I was thinking about this when I heard in my mind, 'Orion is the new archangel you are to work with!'

Though very excited, I was also a little unsure about this – after all, why me? After thinking it over, the next day I said out loud, 'Well, Orion, if you're real and want to work with me, you'd better send me a sign then!' Charming, I know, and I wasn't even getting his name right – the funny thing is I was saying it as in the chocolate cookies Oreos, except with an 'n' on the end.

A week later I had a book-launch party, and as a surprise, my mum asked a cake-maker to create 100 cupcakes for me. They came with stars on them with 'Kyle' embossed on them and mini Oreo cookies on top. I laughed and thought, *Orion, is this a sign? If so, I want you to bring something even better!'*

The party was a great success, with 150 friends, family members, colleagues and clients celebrating with me, and even bringing presents. When I went to my room that night in the hotel, I thought I'd open a couple!

With my close friends around me, I started to look through them. There were some lovely gifts, and I was really moved when I opened up one to find a client who had become a good friend had named a star in my honour. I was close to tears as I read that it was in the southern hemisphere in the part of the sky near... yes, you guessed it, Orion!

I knew then that Orion certainly was an archangel and that he was here to help our planet adjust to the new energy.

Our Life Purpose

Like Chamuel, Orion can also help us when it comes to finding our life purpose. When I first began meditating and connecting to his energy, here's what came through:

> *'Your life purpose doesn't define you – you're defined by love. Love is the only part of you that's real and will continue to exist when your human body is gone. Just because you have to create abundance to live doesn't mean that your career defines your life purpose. Your life purpose is to remember that you're an essence of love. If you can align every thought, action and deed with love, you're living your purpose. Nothing is more important than that.'*

Orion encourages us to align our purpose with compassion, love and trust. When we do this, we begin to manifest various opportunities to serve. Instead of questioning what's going to happen next, we surrender and move with the flow of energy that is coming through us.

The Stellar Gateway

Orion's energy governs the stellar gateway chakra, which is found 12 inches above the head. This energy is not only a chakra but a Milky Way of opportunity! It helps us access wisdom from our angels and guides and see our way forward. Here's how to connect with it:

Visualization for Connecting with the Stellar Gateway

✧ Breathe deeply and just focus on your breath for a few moments, allowing your exhale to be longer than your inhale.

✧ As you relax more and more, imagine a Milky Way of energy above your head. See it swirling like a galaxy.

✧ As you connect with this deep stillness, allow yourself to move into this galaxy. See and feel yourself suspended in time and space as you connect to all that is.

✧ While you are there, you may want to say something along the lines of 'Thank you, universe and angels, for revealing to me what I need to know!' or 'Thank you, God, for reminding me of my true purpose!'

I have always found this type of meditation to be very deep. Whenever I've led students to the stellar gateway chakra, I've always given them time to connect with their deep inner guidance. Remember to trust what you receive if you are in this place, because by focusing on deep but gentle breathing, you are aligning your energy with the divine, and the ego cannot interrupt you.

Open Your Ethereal Angel Wings

When we begin to work with Orion's energy we begin to open what are known as our ethereal angel wings! These represent our work and our connection with the angels. When we connect with them, we break through boundaries and are free.

Spreading our wings is a powerful moment. When our wings are retracted, we allow ourselves to be affected by outside influences, and our false perceptions and other people's insanity can hold us back. When we open our ethereal angel wings, it's as if we break the mould. I always imagine it as wings breaking through plaster or *papier mâché* – they open up and fly free.

In most of the meditations I do, I encourage my students to visualize themselves with wings just like their angels, open and stretched out upwards. It always makes them smile!

As a student of yoga, I'm also aware of how physical exercises can support our growth. I always see yoga as prayer in movement. I go to a local class and say my prayers and affirmations all through my practice. From my practice, I've come up with this little sequence to help you open your ethereal angel wings. It's really helpful, especially if you're non-visual.

- ◎ Stand barefoot if you can with your feet hip-width apart. Have the soles of your feet completely flat on the ground. Gently push your feet into the ground and apart, as if you are separating tiles on the floor.

- ◎ Place your hands together in the prayer position at your heart centre.

- ◎ Touch your heart, your throat and your third eye with your thumbs, all the while keeping your hands in the prayer position.

- ◎ Allow your hands to continue upwards until they are above your crown with your elbows to the side.

- ◎ Continue until they're about 12 inches above your head.

- ◎ Release your arms and allow them to shape wings in the air as they come back down by your sides.

- ◎ Your ethereal wings are now open! Be free!

I do this exercise often, and especially before I speak to audiences. I'm never surprised when people come up to me and say they can see energy swirling around me like a pair of wings. Try it — see how it improves your day!

Connect with Orion

Orion can help us with aligning our energy with the cosmos, connecting with universal and planetary information, aligning our purpose with love, accessing our stellar gateway chakra and opening our ethereal angel wings.

Prayer to Orion

Here's a prayer to welcome Orion's energy into your life:

'Thank you, Archangel Orion, for inspiring me and filling my life with your starry energy.

I am open to receiving your guidance. Thank you for revealing to me what I need to know.

I align all my thoughts and actions with love, knowing that this is the real and infinite part of myself.

I am safe and well, knowing you are with me.

And so it is!'

Orion and Other Archangels

◎ Orion and Ariel are wonderful together for manifesting abundance.

◎ Orion works with Metatron and Sandalphon to help us adapt to spiritual shifts.

⮞ ARCHANGEL RAGUEL ⮜

Archangel Raguel, 'Friend of God', is one of the angels of justice. His role is to bring harmony and balance to situations that are out of control and lack love.

Raguel is a beautiful angel, and I must admit I found it difficult to work out whether his energy was male or female. Angels are said to be androgynous in essence, but I have always seen them as either male or female. Raguel does appear to be male, but has a feminine and soft appearance that complements his subtle energy. I always see him as a pearly white being with a bright orange aura. His face is pale and round, his eyes are deep as the night sky, with silver and white swirls in them, and his white hair is brushed back. He stands with his arms open to his sides and emanates a divine love that brings us to a calm centre.

When I connected to Raguel to understand his role and purpose, here is the message I heard:

'My role is to bring a sense of calm and harmony to situations and places that have forgotten about the light. As an angel of justice, it is my purpose to ensure that these situations are adhering to the spiritual Law of Grace. I am unable to help in a situation unless called upon; however, when it comes to worldly and universal issues I work to the Law of Grace, ensuring light is brought where it is needed.

'I have a particular need to help relationships, especially where families are feeling the strains that can cause rupture and disconnection. I am here to resolve any conflict within the hearts and homes of those involved.

'It is important to say that I am no judge and I cannot determine the outcome of a situation. It is the universe who decides this, I just follow the laws that are in place.'

Raguel is always present in readings when there is a legal case going on. Whenever I pick up his name at the early stages of a session, I know that he wants to help my client feel at ease and focus on harmony. One of the greatest things about Raguel is he won't help you *fight*, he will help you create harmony. Fighting is a product of fear and he is for *love*. Remember, though, that standing your ground is a loving thing to do. If this is the case for you, call on Raguel to support you.

Once I was doing a reading for a lady in Russia and could see Raguel standing beside her in my mind. In his hand he carried the scales of justice. I hadn't even gotten as far as explaining how the reading was going to work when I found myself blurting out, 'Archangel Raguel, the angel of justice, is helping you with your life purpose in law and with finding harmony as you are currently working in a man's world!'

'I can't believe you've said that!' she replied. 'Although I work in a lab at the moment, I'm in my final year of training to be a barrister!'

I knew that that was the perfect role for her, and she felt reassured that this angel of harmony was encouraging her down that path.

Resolving Conflict

Whenever we find ourselves in conflict with another person, we pull all of our energy in and close ourselves off from the divine love and support that is there for us, especially if we begin criticizing the person we're arguing with.

If we want to resolve this conflict, there's a really important question we need to ask ourselves, and it comes from *A Course in Miracles*:

'Would you rather be right or happy?'

If your answer is 'Happy', then Raguel is there to help you. One of the things he mentioned in his message is that he cannot judge, nor can he decide who's right and who's wrong, but what he can do is return a situation to love. So, when we call on him, he will bathe our whole situation in his orange harmonious light.

Connect with Raguel

Raguel can help us with any sort of legal matter, our career if we work in law, bringing balance and harmony to a situation, resolving conflicts or arguments, welcoming and manifesting friends, and moving away from those we can't help any longer.

Prayers to Raguel

Here's a prayer to welcome Raguel's energy into your life:

'Dear Raguel the Archangel,

Thank you for shining your harmonious light of balance on my life.

Thank you for helping me recognize all those who are trustworthy.

Thank you for bringing any conflicts or arguments in my life to an end.

Thank you for helping me discern what is right and what is wrong.

Thank you for being a great friend and shining God's light on me.

It feels so good to know you are here, guiding my path to growth!

And so it is!'

Here's a prayer for calling on Raguel's help in resolving conflict:

'Thank you, Archangel Raguel, for surrounding me, [name of person], *and this situation in a space of harmonious love.*

I surrender this whole situation to you, knowing that from this point on it has already been resolved.

And so it is!'

As *Raguel* means 'Friend of God', Raguel is also absolutely brilliant for any friendship issues, including manifesting new friends. My mother has always told me that you can never have enough friends, and she's absolutely right.

We're always learning and developing, however, and this means that friends will come and go. I feel that they will always reflect our level of development. Some of them will come with great lessons, too. But our challenging friends can be our greatest teachers.

If you're finding it difficult to work out who your friends *really* are, Raguel can help. Try this prayer:

'Dear Raguel, thank you for wrapping your harmonious light around me so that I can feel warm and protected.

I surrender my friendships to you, dear one.

Thank you for illuminating the souls I can trust with confidence and for helping me to let go of those who do not act with integrity.

I do this in the space of love and know that it's best for the growth of all of us.

And so it is!'

If you're ready to manifest new friends who will benefit your growth, try this:

'I now open my heart with love and appreciation to the new souls who are joining me on my journey!

I am so glad to welcome into my life friends and teachers who are constantly improving themselves and their spiritual connection.

Dear Raguel, thank you for directing this whole process!

And so it is!'

Raguel and Other Archangels

◎ Raguel works with Jeremiel to help us recognize the divine harmony behind the illusions of fear.

◎ He also works with Michael to help us detach from drama or from people whose words and actions are harmful.

◎ He works with Michael and Zadkiel to resolve legal issues, and we can ask him and Raziel to come together to uncover information in a legal case that has secrets (remembering to add that all should be for the highest good).

❧ ARCHANGEL RAPHAEL ❧

Archangel Raphael is a beautiful and powerful angel. His name translates as 'God heals', and this special being governs a choir of angels dedicated to health and healing on all levels.

Raphael is well known, especially for his emerald-green aura. He is said to carry a caduceus, the winged staff with twin coiled serpents that is a symbol of the medical profession and is seen on the side of ambulances and on medical uniforms.

I see Raphael as a tall handsome angel with bronze skin and dark curly locks, wearing muscle-moulded copper and gold breastplates. He has bright, almost pearlescent wings and a green-and-gold aura swirling around him. He holds his caduceus, but I see this more as a wand than a staff.

Healing

Raphael is not only dedicated to helping us heal; he wants us to live a healthy lifestyle, too. Some of the most important things he has taught me are to have a balanced diet, to make time to relax and to drink plenty of water.

Raphael can help us when it comes to weight loss, personal fitness and changing old eating habits. His choir of angels is also dedicated to our health and wellbeing. They, like him, are waiting for our call. We can either ask them for healing for ourselves or for others. We can thank them for looking after a loved one who's ill or even someone we don't know at all.

Visualizing an emerald-green light washing over us from head to toe can really bring Raphael's energy to us. When I do it, I imagine that this light not only washes over my body but also penetrates my skull and courses through my veins and every major organ. I see it as a green liquid light that is moving gently through me, doing what it needs to do.

When I was working with Raphael during the writing of this book, I felt inspired to ask for a message on healing. Here's what I received:

> 'Dear one, thank you for taking a great
> interest in the power and miracles of healing.
> It is very important that you know your mind
> is the greatest tool you have to heal yourself.
> Your body is very sensitive to every thought
> you think and every action you perform. It is

controlled by your thoughts and actions, not the other way about. This is why people can spiral downwards so quickly. Be aware that you can influence your body in a positive way. Even when you're well, treat it with love, treat it with respect and it will be stronger on your journey.'

Something that I feel it is important to repeat here is that fighting with a dis-ease isn't the way to go! Remember that love eradicates fear, and fear eradicates love, and dis-ease is a product of fear? So, you know what you need to do, right? *Let love in*!

Love your body, send blessings to it. If you work on the ray of love and send love to your body, it will begin rippling through every cell, encouraging your whole body to resume its natural healthy state.

Guiding Travellers

As well as bringing healing, Raphael can be called upon when we're going on a journey. With his healing ray, he can help us feel comforted and safe while on the move.

Something really amazing happens when we invite Raphael and his angels to travel with us – everything seems to run perfectly. I call on Raphael every time I have a flight ahead or am travelling any distance on the train, and I always feel safe and relaxed, so much so that I'm famous for falling asleep before take-off!

Connect with Raphael

Raphael can help us with healing on all levels, freeing ourselves from addictions or old habits, opening our heart chakra, cleansing our third eye for increasing clairvoyance and feeling safe while travelling.

A Prayer to Raphael

Here's a prayer to welcome Raphael's energy into your life:

'Archangel Raphael, divine healer,

Thank you for your strength and support.

I allow your healing light to wash through every cell of my body.

I acknowledge healing begins in the present and so accept healing now. It feels so good as my body returns to health; it feels amazing knowing I am alive, vital and free.

I remember that only love is real; I focus on the love within that brings me peace of mind and happiness.

I am whole again, I am healed, I am love. With gratitude, I am well!

And so it is!'

Raphael and Other Archangels

© Raphael and Ariel bring healing to the animal kingdom.

© Raphael works with Chamuel to help us see love in a situation.

© He works with Haniel and Raziel to help us cultivate our spiritual gifts and clairvoyance.

© He works with Metatron to clear our body and energy. They're also a great combination to call on if you're a Reiki practitioner.

© He can work with Raziel to help us increase our knowledge of healing.

⤙ ARCHANGEL RAZIEL ⤚

Raziel, the archangel I like to refer to as a 'magician' or 'old sage', is the angel who governs many of the spiritual laws that affect Earth, especially the Law of Manifestation (*see Chapter 4*). His name means 'Secrets of God', and this is because he knows the ins and outs of universal energy.

Raziel appears in many different ways to me. I've seen him with sun-kissed dark skin, looking rather Egyptian. However, I've also seen him as an Indian yogi. I believe he has walked the Earth in many physical bodies to teach us the ways of our beautiful universe.

When we connect with Raziel, his golden aura will wash over us and align our energy with the universe. He can teach us how to understand and work with the spiritual laws to support our growth. He helps us discover the energy of God that flows through us. He can open our mind and help us connect with our inner wisdom.

One of the most important messages that Raziel shares with us is:

> *'Knowledge is learned, whereas wisdom comes from within. As you connect with me and my energy, I will take you on an inner journey on which you can discover the answers you seek. By acknowledging God within, your higher self, you will extend your energy to the universe and begin to see more clearly. Your vision already exists; it just takes that moment when you open your eyes and acknowledge the divine in you, which is then shown throughout your life.'*

We are constantly looking outside ourselves for answers rather than connecting to God, who isn't 'up there' but 'in here', in our heart. Our higher self is our divine intelligence; it's that voice of support and unconditional love that can be seen as the voice of grace, spirit or even angels. Raziel can help you awaken it.

Increase Your Spiritual Knowledge

Raziel has the ability to help us feel at ease, especially when it comes to our spiritual understanding. So many of us can find ourselves 'mind boggled' when it comes to understanding the natural spiritual laws such as Attraction, Manifestation and Karma. When we connect with Raziel, he will help us process and understand the information.

Working with Raziel can also be helpful when learning a system such as the Kabbalah or *A Course in Miracles*, or even gearing up to be a Reiki master. He will help us attune our energies to the teachings and understand them for our growth.

Meditation

Meditation is so important for our awareness and development. Dedicating at least 10 minutes a day five days a week will really help us to attune to the angels and their messages.

If you ever want to learn more and find yourself looking for a new book, new course or new lecture, *stop*! Welcome in Raziel and meditate. The best learning comes when we go within, when we breathe deeply and close our eyes, when we make time to remember who we really are.

Yoga

Doing a physical practice like yoga, where we flow with our body and breathing, can really enhance our spiritual practice, too. Creating that physical alignment of our spine and deepening our breath allows our prayers to soar high to God and enables us to listen to the divine richness of our soul.

Because of the rich knowledge in yoga and the way it connects the soul with the physical body, when we practise it we can particularly enhance our connection to Raziel.

Connect with Raziel

Raziel can help us with understanding and working with the spiritual laws, increasing our spiritual knowledge, learning through meditation and connecting soul and body through yoga.

A Prayer to Raziel

Here's a prayer to welcome Raziel's energy into your life:

> *'Archangel Raziel, the divine magician,*
>
> *Thank you for opening up my mind and heart to spiritual knowledge.*
>
> *I feel so connected, knowing and understanding the universal laws*
>
> *So that I can create the life I deserve.*
>
> *Thank you for blessing my aura with your intelligence,*
>
> *So I can understand myself and my life even more.*
>
> *Thank you for reminding me of my spiritual function and purpose.*

It's so good to travel through life with your knowledge.

And so it is!'

Raziel and Other Archangels

◎ Raziel, Haniel and Raphael help us cultivate our spiritual gifts and clairvoyance.

◎ Raziel and Jophiel can deepen our awareness and still the mind in meditation.

◎ We can ask Raziel and Raguel to come together to uncover information in a legal case that has secrets (remembering to add that all should be for the highest good).

◎ Raziel and Raphael work together to help us increase our healing knowledge.

~ ARCHANGEL SANDALPHON ~

Archangel Sandalphon, the angel of the Earth, is the twin brother of Metatron. Just like him he once walked the Earth, in his case as the biblical prophet Elijah. Now he connects us to the heart of Mother Earth and helps us obtain information and insight from her.

Sandalphon has a lovely copper aura. He is a beautiful, pale-faced, almost feminine-looking angel, but has a muscular body. Music is often heard when he arrives. His wingspan is huge, and when you call upon him he will wrap his wings around you to make you feel safe.

Sandalphon's name can mean a few different things. It is very similar to the Greek word *synadelfos*, which means 'co-worker', but many also believe it could mean 'co-brother', as *adelphos* is Greek for 'brother'. The brother connection could definitely work, given that he and Metatron are twins.

The Master of Song

Sandalphon is the master of song and loves music. When we listen to music, it raises our spirits and lifts our consciousness up to heaven. Not only that, it affects our heart and circulation and can have a therapeutic effect on the body. If you're a budding musician or want to demonstrate your talents at singing or playing an instrument, Sandalphon will support you.

The Angel Who Delivers Our Prayers to Heaven

During Moses' visit to the third heaven, he is said to have seen Sandalphon and referred to him as 'the tall angel', although this idea goes back to before the Torah. In the Babylonian Talmud, Sandalphon's head reaches heaven. The way I interpret this is that if Sandalphon's feet are on Earth and his head is in heaven, he is delivering our prayers to the creator.

I have also read that in the liturgy for the Jewish Feast of Tabernacles Sandalphon is acknowledged for gathering the prayers of the faithful and creating a garland from them to present to 'the king of kings', or God.

To this day, Sandalphon carries our prayers like a divine postman, making sure God gets our special delivery. Through synchronicity, he can also indicate the answers we're looking for. If you're having trouble finding answers to your prayers, he's your man.

Finding a Lost Item

Sandalphon works with the copper ray, which is the energy that allows us to connect with Mother Earth, or as I call her, Gaia. It is a spiritual light we can visualize in order to connect with the energies and intelligence of our planet. When we do this, Gaia can direct us on our path and give us guidance on how we can help humanity.

If we visualize the copper light beneath our feet, we can see it extending to parts of the world that need extra energy, love, compassion and healing. It is an energy that is infinite, but according to the Law of Free Will, we have to give it permission to go out and heal.

As copper is also a metal, Sandalphon has many close connections to the planet and can therefore help us find material things, too. Through prayer you can call upon him and thank him for directing you to something you're looking for.

I remember my mother once had a lovely slice of rose quartz that was hidden away somewhere not being used. It was a rectangular piece that was polished on one side and around the same size as my angel card deck. I'd been asking her for a few weeks to find it, as I really wanted to use it in my work, and she kept putting me off, saying she wasn't sure where it was. Then one night I said, 'Mum, have you found that slice of rose quartz yet?'

'Oh, for goodness' sake, I'll look for it now. Will you please stop going on?!'

I began to laugh at her diva fit, but not too hard, as I really did want the rose quartz.

Mum said out loud, 'Thank you, Archangel Sandalphon, for showing me where this rose quartz is!'

Then out of nowhere she had a vision that the rose quartz was in her wardrobe in a box underneath a pile of books.

'I know where it is!' she called out and ran to her room, where, sure enough, she found the large crystal slice.

My mother claims she's not psychic and doesn't want to be, and that she just saw the rose quartz as you would in a daydream. Calling on Sandalphon to find a lost item can help you locate it through your natural intuition. But however you do it, do call on him and look out for amazing results.

The Earth Star Chakra

The Earth star chakra is an anchor to the Earth in the shape of a large crystal star 12 inches below our feet. When we connect to this energy, we ground ourselves and come right back down to Earth but still maintain our connection to heaven.

This beautiful chakra can help us send healing to the planet, connect to it to gain wisdom, and walk through life feeling connected to joy and to our pathway. The best way to connect with it is through visualization and affirmation. Though it is 12 inches below our feet, because it helps us connect with the Earth, I always get people to imagine it at the very centre of the Earth:

Visualization for Connecting with Your Earth Star

✧ Imagine your feet growing the most amazing gold and copper roots that go right down to the centre of the Earth.

✧ When they reach the centre, they find a large crystal star there and wrap themselves around it. Tie them around it so tightly and so strongly that you anchor yourself right into the Earth.

✧ Then take several deep breaths and remain open to anything you're shown or told, as we can be given so much insight by Sandalphon, and, of course, the Earth herself.

Another great way to connect to your Earth star is with this affirmation:

'I am grounded and centred. I root myself to the Earth. I am the Earth and the Earth is me. I align with my Earth star. We are one'.

Here's a message from Sandalphon:

> *'Work with me and my light to connect and bond with the infinite wisdom of our great mother, planet Earth. Plant your feet firmly on her soil and download her exquisite intelligence, which is being offered to you now. When you connect to both heaven and Earth through your mind, you suspend yourself in a protective cocoon of love that flows freely from both of these dimensions. It is time to bond with the Earth so that you know the way forward from here!'*

Connect with Sandalphon

Sandalphon can help us with channelling our creativity through music, finding a lost item, connecting to the Earth for support and grounding, sending our prayers to heaven (think of him as a heavenly postman!) and understanding signs and synchronicities.

A Prayer to Sandalphon

> *'Archangel Sandalphon, Angel of the Earth,*
> *I welcome your copper light into my life.*
>
> *Thank you for guiding me to understand the signs of heaven's presence and for delivering my prayers to heaven.*

I allow myself to become connected with you and the intelligence of planet Earth.

Dear Sandalphon, remind me how I can serve, how I can shine, and how I can adjust to the planetary changes going on. I surrender to your force!

And so it is!'

Sandalphon and Other Archangels

- © Sandalphon and Chamuel can work together so we can intuitively find our soul mate on Earth.

- © Sandalphon works with Metatron to ensure we can have a spiritual connection without having to lose our balance as a 'human'.

- © He also works with Metatron and Orion to help us adapt to the spiritual shifts that are taking place on the planet.

- © Sandalphon and Uriel are a great team for helping us get answers to our prayers and to solve problems.

☙ ARCHANGEL URIEL ☙

Uriel is one of the four main archangels mentioned in Abrahamic texts. His name comes from the Hebrew for 'God's light' and I call him 'the angel of light'. He is a powerful angel with a sunny nature who lights up any type of darkness. When I connect with him, he reminds me of the sun – ever glowing, bright and warm.

My clairvoyant view of Uriel is as a tall, handsome pale-skinned angel with a bright yellow-and-gold aura. His eyes are deep blue like the night sky, and his body is covered in golden armour. He carries a torch of light.

Uriel can help us in many ways. He brings us inspiration and creative thoughts. He is particularly brilliant at helping us obtain answers to questions and is great for problem-solving, too. Anytime we are unsure about a decision, we can welcome in Uriel to help us make the right choice.

I've found that Uriel is absolutely amazing for those who are self-employed or thinking of running their own business. This is because he helps us think quickly and know what to do and where we're going. If you're creative and need some inspiration, Uriel can help you unlock your gifts and move to the next level. He will encourage your unique gifts, inspire you to grow, and help your business gain recognition.

I always feel that Uriel's energy is like spending a day in the outdoors, with fresh air, clear blue skies and warm sunshine. After days like this we feel uplifted and happy. Uriel brings the joy of life, the light of heaven and divine inspiration.

Here is a message from him:

'I am the light of God that shines through your heart and mind. Call on me to illuminate the path ahead so you can clearly see how you can create change and balance in your life. By trusting in me and the angels of light, you will be of great service to humanity. Remember that being of service and shining God's light will not only help others grow but increase your divine connection, too.'

The Angels of Light

Uriel has a team of angels whom I call 'the angels of light'. These angels are dedicated to the soul of the Earth. They can be called upon when there is any sort of disaster or tragic circumstance that really needs truth and light. Whenever you are aware of a situation that needs great healing and light, call upon Uriel and the angels of light to illuminate all involved. They will be there for everything from tsunamis to earthquakes, floods, terrorist activity and tragic accidents.

Here is a prayer to call on Uriel and the angels of light:

'Archangel Uriel and the angels of light, thank you so much for casting your light over [the situation] *and all those involved. Remind them of your presence and illuminate them so that they find comfort and peace. Thank you for lovingly directing all you can to safety and peace. And so it is!'*

Men's Health

Uriel is closely connected to the male aspect of health and wellbeing – everything from prostate issues to fertility. As he works with the energy of the sun, which in many traditions is the symbol of God and the male aspect of the universe, he will be able to restore life-force, energy and, of course, much-needed stamina. I always recommend a prayer to Uriel to boost the libido and the ability to create life.

The angels are aware of the importance of sexual health and wellbeing, so there's no need for embarrassment. If you know someone who's experiencing issues here, call on Uriel for illumination and balance.

Connect with Uriel

Uriel can help us with starting a business, being creative, problem-solving, illuminating a dark situation and men's health and fertility issues.

A Prayer to Uriel

Here's a prayer to welcome Uriel's energy into your life:

'Archangel Uriel, Light of God,

I am open to your guidance and support. Thank you for enabling me to recognize my inner light and creativity and for illuminating the path ahead.

I open my spiritual eyes and allow my higher self to take me forward, following your promptings. I allow myself to shine, knowing I deserve only the best.

Thank you, Uriel, for reminding me of your presence and for helping me realize I have gifts to share with this planet.

And so it is!'

Uriel and Other Archangels

© Uriel works with Chamuel on career issues.

© Uriel and Sandalphon are a great team for helping us get answers to our prayers and solve problems.

⮑ ARCHANGEL ZADKIEL ⮐

Zadkiel is a powerful archangel whose name translates as 'Righteousness of God'. He is one of the justice angels, along with Michael and Raguel.

Zadkiel has an amazing deep purple and ultraviolet aura with a really purifying energy. When I see him clairvoyantly, he reminds me of A. C. Slater from the teenage sitcom *Saved by the Bell*. He has a mixed-race appearance, with golden skin and a muscular build.

I have nicknamed him 'the peacekeeper', as he comes to help us forgive and have compassion for those who have created challenges for us in our life. He is almost like the inner voice of grace – he wants us all to love each other and is dedicated to helping us put things right when they go wrong. He encourages us to find compassion for both ourselves and others. He is an angel of balance who can help us to become merciful and find deep inner peace.

Keeper of the Violet Flame

Zadkiel is the keeper of the violet flame, a spiritual energy that helps us to release anything from our past that is holding us back. We can take everything from relationships to traumatic experiences and even past-life challenges to the violet flame, knowing it will transmute pain into love and have a hugely positive effect on our life and energy.

The most amazing thing about the violet flame is that even though it will release all negativity and trauma, it won't affect anything that is already good. For example, you and your partner are having issues in your relationship. There are some great aspects to your bond, but a financial issue is coming between you. When you present your relationship to Zadkiel and the violet flame, they will energetically release you from the burdens and fear, transform any arguments into compassion and, most of all, create space for your love to grow.

Sometimes things you least expect come to your mind when you connect with the violet flame – half-forgotten situations from your childhood, or memories that aren't even from this life. Surrender to the process and trust that Zadkiel is releasing everything that you don't need in your life now.

You can connect with the violet flame through visualization or affirmation.

Visualization for Connecting with the Violet Flame

✧ Imagine going into a room in heaven with a large fire pit in the centre. Bright ultraviolet flames burn at the heart of the fire.

✧ As you stand by those flames, think of any situations you are ready to let go of or ask to be shown what you need to release.

✧ Turn these situations into bundles of wood and place them on the ultraviolet flames.

✧ See them being completely consumed by the energy of the flames and say, 'I surrender this issue to the violet flame in the presence of Archangel Zadkiel!'

There is something so powerful about saying 'I am', then naming a form of energy. When we affirm we are the violet flame, we bring it into ourselves and allow it to work through our body. This will enable us to release all that we no longer need, and will target everything from past lives to childhood memories and present issues without our having to be fully conscious of them. Try this:

'I am the violet flame of purification.

I surrender and release all fear from my being.

Transmute and transform, compassion fulfil me,

*I am showered in mercy and now I am set free!
And so it is!'*

Here's a message from Zadkiel:

*'Working with me shows your willingness to let
go all that no longer serves you — all the karma
and old habits that have built up over lifetimes
and no longer serve your energy or purpose.
Invoke my presence and my violet light to
transmute this karma and transform old habits
into positive new pathways to follow. The
spiritual power you seek is hidden under these
layers of unneeded fear — it's time to let go!'*

Angels of Justice

Zadkiel works with Michael, Raguel and a force of
angels to bring about justice and compassion to
situations that need it. Whenever I see Zadkiel and
Raguel come up in a reading, I know that there's a legal
situation literally on the cards.

So many people worry about situations like this,
and of course they want the turn-out to go in their
favour. As much as that would be nice, Zadkiel and the
angels of justice will always work for balance and the
highest good of everyone involved.

Karma

If you've been involved in a legal matter and have actually created the situation, remember that everything you do creates a wave and it will come back to you.

Karma is the law of cause and effect. Every single thought you have and action you take will have some sort of effect on you and your life. If you perform a good deed, it will come back to you, and it's the same with things that aren't so positive.

One of the important things about karma is that you *can't* direct it. So many times I've heard people say to someone, 'I hope karma comes back and gets you for that!' It's really important to know you are not a lord of karma and you can't choose how it will work. I always encourage people to leave other people's actions to them and concentrate on their own journey.

Mercy

Wanting bad karma or punishment for someone isn't merciful, and angels always encourage us to have compassion for others, or at the very least for ourselves. When we think negative thoughts about someone, we're really attacking ourselves, because we're all connected – we're all God's children.

When we say someone has held us back or ruined our happiness, we're giving them our power. It's exactly the same when we resent someone and can't find it in our heart to forgive. Remember we have many choices in life, and we choose when to release something and when to hold on to it.

Many people say that they can't forgive because that means they're condoning the negative action. But angels want to remind us that there are only two states of being: *fear* and *love*. When we harm someone else, we're living in fear. When we can't forgive, we're living in fear, too. We're not transcending the situation.

When we focus on love and practise it daily, however, we do transcend the situation. When we send love to the person who's harmed us, that's even better, for if they discover the miracle of love, they can't harm anyone any more.

So, forgiveness doesn't mean we think a negative action is acceptable; it means we're focusing on the one thing that eradicates fear: *love*.

Connect with Zadkiel

Zadkiel can help us with connecting to the violet flame, bringing justice to a legal situation, releasing contracts and karma, connecting to the spirit of mercy and finding it in our heart to forgive.

A Prayer to Zadkiel

Here's a prayer to welcome Zadkiel's energy into your life:

'Archangel Zadkiel, Angel of Justice and Righteousness, Keeper of the Violet Flame,

Thank you for bringing your energy to me now.

I surrender, release and transmute all old karma, contracts and setbacks with love.

I am the violet flame.

The spirit of mercy fills my very core as I find it within myself to forgive and release the past and to focus on compassion.

I am an expression of divine love. Thank you for supporting me.

And so it is!'

Zadkiel and Other Archangels

- ◎ Zadkiel and Michael can help us overcome fears or phobias.

- ◎ Zadkiel, Michael and Azrael are a powerful combination for transmuting and removing fear from a space or home.

- ◎ Zadkiel works with Michael and Raguel to bring about justice.

❧ THE DIVINE MOTHER MARY ❧

Mary, the Divine Mother of Jesus, is Queen of the Angels. She was given that title because when she went to heaven, she continued to be of service to our beautiful planet and she has a strong connection with angels, especially Archangel Michael, as they are both connected to the blue ray of protection and strength.

Although Mary is closely associated with Christianity, in particular the Catholic Church, it is important to say that her energy is non-denominational. She has a special bond with mothers and children, but can be called upon by anyone. I feel that because so many people do acknowledge her and call upon her, thank her, and light candles to her, her energy is almost as powerful as that of the angels themselves.

She definitely has one of the purest hearts I've ever experienced. Every time I connect to energy or see her in a session, I get highly emotional. Her energy is unconditional and loving, and her one wish for humanity is for us to find peace.

Don't worry if you haven't paid much attention to Mary in the past — she won't hold it against you and will be willing to support you from this point onwards.

I'll never forget some of the experiences I've had when I've connected to the Divine Mother and felt her presence. One of them happened soon after I first learned about angels, at around the age of 15.

At that time I used to do readings online for free. Every week I would meditate with my angel cards in hand and pick some to use for a weekly message. This particular day my mum was out at work when I did it. I welcomed in the angels and asked 'anyone else who can help' to come through with guidance for me to share.

As I sat there with my eyes closed, focusing on my breathing, I imagined a golden light swirling around me and protecting me. As I did this, I imagined a rose opening up at my heart centre to represent my heart opening to love.

For some time I just sat in this powerful light, knowing I was connected to God and the angels. Then, out of nowhere or so it seemed, I felt a presence behind me. I instinctively knew it was female. The energy was so emotional and loving, every hair on my body stood on end.

Then a voice began to give me the following message:

'Tell them, tell mothers and children, that I am here to protect them. Encourage them to trust in my love and trust in me. I will lead all those in need from danger and help them feel safe.'

At first I was too busy remembering the message to think about who was relaying it to me, but then in my mind I saw an image of the Divine Mother. She was draped in blue robes as depicted in traditional Catholic imagery, and there was a golden aura around her. I barely saw the colour of her skin or any more details, because her light was so strong. But I knew I had to share her message!

That was all very well, but how was I to do it? I was a 15-year-old kid – no one was going to listen to me, were they?

First of all, I decided to tell my parents about my experience. My mum tried to protect me and wanted me to keep it to myself, but I felt I had to pass it on.

At the time my dad was friends with a lady who was a practicing Catholic, so he asked for advice. She told him that if I went to a local chapel they would record my message and share it. Supposedly there was a register of visitations from 'Our Lady', as she called her.

My dad came to pick me up at my mum's house and took me to a local chapel. The priest welcomed us into his home and began to ask me how Mother Mary had come to me. Had I invited her?

He wrote down the message, but at the end he said I was 'probably just dreaming'. At the time I felt saddened – he wasn't respecting the message. Maybe it was something he already knew, but the Divine Mother wanted to be called upon a lot more....

In the years since then, I've shared that message with as many people as possible and have never felt it's been too late to do so. I feel that more and more people need to know of the support that angels and heaven can offer us. Now I have a platform to share the message; please share it with others.

Domestic Abuse

Every time I have a case where a woman is being mistreated by her husband, partner or even child, I bring in Mother Mary. When she comes into the space, it changes everything. She pours out her divine love and protection like an elixir of life.

Mary protects those who need to get away from domestic abuse and works tirelessly to lead them to safety. If you've suffered from anything like this, or know anyone who has, call on the Divine Mother for assistance. She works with Archangel Michael to bring extra protection to the situation and will help you cut the cords of fear that hold you back from making the change you need.

Here's a message from the angels for those dealing with domestic abuse:

'You always have a voice and you are asked to feel empowered today. It is time you left behind those old ways and moved forward fearlessly. If you work with us and the Divine Mother, we will lead you to safety. Everything you need will be provided if you trust us and make the leap. Only you can do it, but we can help you – you aren't alone!'

Child Protection

Mother Mary also comes to children, especially if they need protection from abuse or danger. She nurtures children who have suffered badly and wants them to be loved as they deserve.

Whenever I see a child who could really do with a boost of love, I thank Mary for going to them, for loving them and for helping them find peace.

Here's a prayer for sending Mary to a child:

Mary, the Divine Mother, thank you for wrapping your light and energy around [child's

name] *and for gently guiding them to safety.*
They are protected and loved in your energy
and I am so grateful you are there for them!
Blessed be!'

Roses

Mother Mary has a strong connection to roses. Whenever I smell them, I think of her or know she is near. Rose is connected to the heart, it represents opening to divine and unconditional love – everything that Mary stands for. By working with roses, you will strengthen your connection to her.

I have my own candle range, and when I created a Mother Mary candle, I knew it had to be made with pure rose essential oil. I have it burning as I write this book today.

Lighting Candles for Peace

There's something very powerful about lighting candles when you say your prayers. I always see it as a boost of energy, a dedication. A candle is something physical that can burn, extending the length of your prayer.

If you feel called to light candles in your home, or even in church, why not say this prayer in support?

'As I light this candle, I create a light in the world. I create peace within myself and allow this to be carried out into this planet.

*Thank you, Divine Mother Mary, for sending
your light of compassion, peace, and love to
all those who need it. I am so grateful you
are the light that guides them to peace, and I
surrender all I can to you, knowing your light
will guide us.*

And so it is!'

Connect with the Divine Mother Mary

Mary can help us with opening our heart to love,
sending love and nurturing to a child and protection
from domestic abuse.

Prayers to Mary

Here's a prayer to welcome Mary's energy into your life:

'Divine Mother Mary, Queen of the Angels,

*Thank you for bestowing your blessings upon my
life.*

*I open my heart to your nurturing light and
energy.*

Thank you for lovingly directing me,

So I can serve humanity just as you do.

*I feel whole, strong and centred, full of deep inner
peace,*

Knowing you and your angels are with me.

And so it is!'

When I was looking through a collection of prayers to the Divine Mother Mary, I found this traditional Catholic prayer to her:

*'We turn to you for protection, Holy Mother
of God. Listen to our prayers and help us in
our needs. Save us from every danger, glorious
and blessed Virgin.'*

I felt this was a beautiful prayer, but it was still seeking help in the future, and we know there's nothing more powerful than the *present moment*, so I have given it an 'angel prayers' revamp:

*'Divine Holy Mother Mary, thank you for
hearing my prayers and helping us with our
needs. I am so grateful for your protection
and comfort at this time and feel so blessed
to know your glorious light is with me! And so
it is!'*

The Divine Mother Mary and Archangels

© Mary works with Gabriel on child, inner child and conception issues.

© She works with Michael to offer protection.

✧ ANGEL AFFIRMATIONS ✧

As mentioned earlier, when we say 'I am' and then a word, we bring the energy connected with that word to us. This can be really valuable when it comes to invoking angels. By saying 'I am' then the angel's name, we bring their whole essence to us.

The other thing we can do is incorporate an archangel's name and energy into an affirmation to bring that extra boost of angelic help.

Here are some archangel affirmations to try:

- ◎ '*I am Ariel*' brings us strength and courage and connects us to animals.

- ◎ '*I am Azrael*' creates a supportive, comforting light around us as we go through a dramatic change or transition.

- ◎ '*I am Chamuel*' helps us to see love.

- ◎ '*I am Gabriel*' supports us in speaking our truth with integrity.

© *'I am Haniel'* allows us to acknowledge our gifts with grace.

© *'I am Jeremiel'* encourages us to tap into the miracle mindset as we evaluate our life and resolve anything that needs to be healed.

© *'I am Jophiel'* shifts our energy to a space where we can see our own beauty and that of the world around us.

© *'I am Metatron'* raises our vibration so we can hear heaven's guidance clearly.

© *'I am Michael'* installs the protection of Archangel Michael in our aura.

© *'I am Orion'* helps us to connect to the cosmos for insight and clarity.

© *'I am Raguel'* helps us create a harmonious and friendly energy to heal any conflict around us.

© *'I am Raphael'* brings the healing rays of God into our aura.

© *'I am Raziel'* helps us understand spiritual and esoteric information.

© *'I am Sandalphon'* connects us to the divine wisdom that flows through us.

- '*I am Uriel*' connects our mind to God's light, enabling us to find the answers we seek.

- '*I am Zadkiel*' shows us the right thing to do!

Affirmations incorporating angels:

- 'I speak my truth with ease, knowing Archangel Gabriel's strength is with me.'

- 'I am safe and protected by the light of Archangel Michael.'

- 'My body is whole and healed in the light of Archangel Raphael.'

- 'I am inspired and directed by the light of Archangel Uriel.'

PART III

DIRECTORY OF PRAYERS

✧ INTRODUCTION ✧

Prayer can be incorporated into every experience of our life. We can pray to give thanks for our food, for the birth of a child or to encourage healing to take place in our body. No matter what our reason for praying, it's always useful because we welcome in the higher powers, open ourselves up, and prepare for divine order to balance our situation.

In the following pages you'll find a selection of prayers that have been categorized so that you can have easy access to those that will support you whenever you need them.

In the first section I have listed prayers to enhance your daily routine. In the next section every other issue should be listed, or something close to it, giving you inspiration and encouraging you to harness heaven's help.

✎ DAILY PRAYERS ✎

Guardian Angel Prayers

Here are five short prayers to your guardian angels:

> *'Thank you, angels, for surrounding me in your light. I surrender my day to you, knowing only good lies before me!'*

> *'Divine angels, I let go and allow your wings to take me forward today. Thank you!'*

> *'Angels surround my day in their light. I know I am loved and protected!'*

> *'Thank you, angels, for protecting me today. It's good to know you're there.'*

> *'Thank you, angels, for reminding me of your presence!'*

Daily Routine Prayers

Beginning your day on a positive note is one of the most important things you can do. Louise Hay, the founder of Hay House publishers, recently said, 'The way you start your day is how you live your day!' and she's absolutely right. If you want to improve the quality of your life, it is essential you open your day to the divine and go through it with a sense of gratitude.

Waking Up

'Thank you, angels and the universe, for filling my body with vitality and energy. It's so good to be alive! As I begin my day, I acknowledge the divine inside me and know that this is a great day! And so it is!'

In the Shower/Bath

'Thank you, heaven, for allowing this water to have a cleansing effect on my body. As I rinse/ soak my skin, I release all that I no longer need and replace it with love, acceptance and your light. I am safe and strong!'

Being on Time (Especially If You're Running Late)

'Thank you, Archangel Metatron and angels of time, for supporting me and getting me back on track. I know that everything is on time and it is perfect. All roadblocks ahead are cleared as I create a positive day ahead! And so it is!'

Giving Thanks for Your Food

*'Thank you, God and angels, for the food that
I am about to eat. It is filled with light and
nutrition that is fulfilling my body's needs. I am
so blessed and healthy. And so it is!'*

Cleaning the House and Cleansing Its Energy

*'Thank you, heaven, for surrounding my home in
your light. As I sweep and clean away the dust,
I allow you to replace it with love and serenity.
I cleanse the soul of my home and I am at peace
here. And so it is!'*

Boosting Your Energy Through the Day

*'Thank you, angels and Archangel Uriel, for
filling my whole being with vitality. I light up like
the sun and express my joy at being alive!'*

∽ A–Z DIRECTORY ∽
OF PRAYERS

A

Abundance

Abundance is defined as 'a lot of something', but when we speak about it with angels, it represents financial income, the fulfilment of material and spiritual needs and a sense of purpose. Abundance is a quality of spirit, and it is natural to receive it. If you are living a life you love, then you have abundance.

Creating

'Divine angels of abundance, I am so grateful for the continued opportunities to create abundance in my life right now. Thank you for directing me to more!'

Increasing

'Thank you, angels, for the blessings in my life. I open my arms to receive the abundance I know I deserve!'

Animals

Call on Archangel Ariel, the angel of animals, to guide and protect pets and wildlife. She works with Michael for extra protection and Azrael when animals are crossing over.

Healing for Animals

'Thank you, Ariel, Raphael and angels, for surrounding [pet's name] *in your healing light. I am so grateful for their health and that you are guiding them to wellness. Your light allows them to feel comforted and safe. All is well in their world for the highest good. And so it is!'*

Lost Animals

'Thank you, Ariel and angels, for lovingly directing [animal's name] *home. I know that they'll be safe under your watch and am so grateful to be reunited with them. I surrender my concerns about this situation to you, knowing that the highest good for all will be created. And so it is!'*

Protecting Animals

'Ariel, Michael and divine angels, thank you for wrapping your wings around [animal's name] *at this time. Allow them to feel comforted and strong. Lead them to safety and guide them to happiness. I surrender this situation to you. And so it is!'*

Supporting an Animal as It Crosses Over

'Thank you, Ariel, Azrael, and the angels of light, for lovingly guiding this divine animal home. It's now time for them to return! They are safe in your light!'

Wildlife

'Thank you, Ariel, for spreading your light around this animal [mention its situation] and leading it to safety! All is well under the Law of Grace!'

Arguments and Other Conflicts

Call on Archangel Raguel to bring peace and harmony to any conflict.

Creating Peace

'Thank you, angels of peace, for surrounding this situation with your light. Raguel, I am so grateful you are guiding all involved to harmony! And so it is!'

Letting Go

'Dear Archangel Raguel, I lovingly release this situation to you and know that from this moment onward it has been taken care of. And so it is!'

Resolution

'Thank you, Raguel and the angels of peace, for resolving this situation. I remember that only love is real and allow this to create a wave of good energy that washes over all involved. And so it is!'

Assertiveness
Increasing

'Thank you, angels, for unlocking my assertiveness. I am strong and courageous and have the ability to stand my ground because I know you're with me now. I am filled with integrity as I affirm that I am safe! And so it is!'

B

Bereavement
(See Grieving.)

C

Career

Archangels Chamuel and Uriel are the career angels. Chamuel is known for helping us regain a love for life and sense of purpose. Uriel is the angel who lights up the darkness, helping us find inspiration.

Dealing with Difficult Colleagues

'Thank you, Chamuel and angels, for surrounding this situation and everyone involved in a space of love. I surrender it to you, knowing that balance and harmony resolve all conflicts now!'

Finding Employment

'Thank you, Uriel and angels, for guiding me to a career that fulfils my every need. I feel so blessed, knowing I have a sense of purpose!'

Fulfilling Your Purpose

'Thank you, Chamuel and Uriel, for guiding me to find my purpose and inspiring me to continue on my chosen path! I feel alive and inspired, shining my light out into the world!'

Promotion

'Dear angels, I am so grateful for this promotion and step forward into a happy and abundant lifestyle. I'm just so passionate about my career and know I can carry out this role to the best of my ability!'

Chakras

When called upon, Archangel Metatron uses his magenta and crystalline rays to balance and cleanse the chakras.

Balancing

'Thank you, Metatron, for allowing your rays of light to balance and strengthen my chakras. I feel so alive and aligned, knowing my spiritual energy is in balance. And so it is!'

Cleansing

'Dear Metatron, thank you for cleansing my energy centres with your crystalline ray. I know now that they have shifted, correcting any blocks or leaks, and that they are moving into a natural flow and balance. And so it is!'

Children

Archangels Gabriel and Metatron are the angels of children. Gabriel is a mothering, nurturing angel, and Metatron supports highly sensitive and creative children. Raphael, the healing angel, can also support children whose health needs a boost, and Michael can protect children. The Divine Mother Mary also supports children.

Adoption

'Thank you, Archangel Gabriel and angels, for bringing into our life a child we can love, support and guide toward a happy and loved life! We are so grateful to parent someone who deserves a second chance!'

Birth

'Thank you, Archangel Gabriel and Mother Mary, for supporting me as I give birth to my child. Thank you for surrounding us in a harmonious healing light, and for allowing us to be with those who will support our health and wellbeing. And so it is!'

Conceiving

For a woman:

'Dear Archangel Gabriel and angels, I am so thankful for this opportunity to produce a child. My maternal instincts are in place, and I'm so thankful for my bundle of joy!

For a man:

'Dear Archangel Gabriel and angels, thank you for supporting us as we bring a new life into this world. It gives us great pleasure to bring a new soul to this Earth! This child is nurtured and loved!'

Direction

'Thank you, Archangel Metatron, for lovingly directing [child's name] *in life and helping them to have confidence and see their unlimited potential! I surrender this situation to you, all for the highest good! And so it is!'*

Healing

'Thank you, Gabriel, Raphael, and angels, for surrounding [child's name] *in healing, nurturing light. We are so grateful for their full recovery to health. It's a joy for them to live and we surrender this situation to you, knowing the best outcome is created!'*

Protecting

'Thank you, Metatron, Michael and angels, for surrounding [child's name] *in protective light! We know they are safe as you wrap your light and wings around them!'*

Creativity

Archangel Uriel, the angel of light, helps us unleash our creative talents.

Expressing

'Thank you, angels of creativity, for allowing me to tap into my creative gifts and talents. I feel so inspired and energized as I allow my gifts to shine!'

Compassion

'Thank you, angels, for allowing me to see [name person/situation] in a more loving and compassionate way. I know that by serving another person, I am opening my heart to unconditional love. And so it is!'

(See also Archangel Zadkiel.)

D

Decisions

Making the Right Decision

'Thank you, angels, for lovingly directing me to the best outcome of this situation. I allow my intuition to guide me to what's right for all involved! And so it is!'

Detoxification

'Thank you, Raphael and healing angels, for supporting me as I release what no longer serves my purpose and body. I take this conscious decision to fill my whole being with healthy energy! I am safe and strong!'

Divorce

Call on Raguel and Zadkiel, the angels of justice, to help you release the energetic ties and create harmony as you and a partner go separate ways.

Creating Harmony

'Archangel Raguel, divine angel of justice, thank you for surrounding me and [ex-partner] *in a space of harmony. I allow a wave of serenity from within to wash over this soul and their life as I bid them a pleasant farewell! And so it is!'*

Dissolving a Marriage Ceremony

'Thank you, Archangel Zadkiel, for allowing my marriage with [person] *to be dissolved. With the violet flame I transmute any grievances and grudges as I set myself free with love. I am filled with compassion and mercy as I move forward, fearlessly supported by the mind of God. And so it is!'*

(See also Relationships.)

Dreams

Connecting with Angels via Dreams

'Thank you, dear angels, for sending me messages of love and support through my dreams. Thank you for blessing my dreams with your presence and allowing our connection to grow even stronger. I feel so inspired, and love knowing you're with me!'

Protection from Nightmares

'Dear Archangel Michael and angels of God, thank you for entering my heart and for protecting me during sleep. I feel so safe and relaxed knowing your love is guiding me into a deep sleep filled with love and inspiration. And so it is!'

Remembering Dreams

'Angels of dreamland, thank you for supporting me in remembering and learning from my dreams. I allow myself to tap into the hidden knowledge and wisdom they hold for me. And so it is!'

E

Ego

Sending the Ego Love

'Angels of divine love, thank you for sending my ego your light and for reminding me that only love is real. By aligning my thoughts with yours, I allow my intuition to be divinely guided!'

Silencing Your Ego Voice

'Thank you, angels, for silencing the voice of my ego so I can hear my intuition and divine intelligence. And so it is!'

(See also Archangel Jophiel.)

Emergencies

Creating Safety

'Thank you, angels of protection, for lovingly guiding all those in this situation [hold thought on situation] *to safety. I release this to you in the Law of Grace, knowing you will do what's best. And so it is!'*

Earth Disasters

'Dear angels of God, healing and grace, thank you for surrounding our divine planet in your light. Thank you for supporting all of those in need and for creating a wave of harmony and healing in all places you can. I surrender this to you knowing you will do the best all for the highest good!'

Getting Help

'Thank you, angels, for directing those who can best help and heal this situation to it! I know you will inspire and direct those who can be of great service to healing and creating balance again. And so it is!'

F

Faith

Increasing

'Thank you, dear angels, for allowing me to see, hear and feel more clearly so I can increase not only my faith in you but also my faith in myself.

*Thank you, God, for constantly reminding me
of your presence in my life. I know I don't travel
this journey alone and I'm grateful that my
angel companions are with me and that you are
in my heart!'*

Family

*'Thank you, angels of peace, for surrounding my
family in your serene light and guiding us to where
we all need to be!'*

Female Issues

Archangels Ariel and Haniel have particularly strong
bonds with women and can support you in tapping
into your inner goddess and in any situation in which
you need support or healing.

Increasing Femininity

*'Dear Archangel Haniel and angels, thank you for
allowing me to see and believe that being a strong
and centred woman is a part of who I am. Thank
you, Ariel, for giving me the courage to express my
femininity so that I can shine from the inside out.
And so it is!'*

Menopause

*'Dear Haniel, thank you for guiding me to the
next cycle of womanhood, I lovingly accept these
natural changes in my body as a symbol of my
growth and development in life. It is a joy to be*

a woman and to move into the next phase of my journey. I feel strong and empowered, knowing you are guiding me through. And so it is!'

PMS

'Thank you, Archangel Haniel, for allowing me to adapt to the natural cycles of my body and thank you, Raphael the healer, for comforting me through this time. I know my body is a safe place to be. And so it is!'

Standing Strong

'Thank you, Archangel Ariel, Lioness of God, for supporting me as I stand strong for what I believe in. I allow my soul to fill up with your courageous light as I speak my truth today!'

Finances

Emergency Cash Flow

'Dear angels, I surrender my financial situation to you, knowing my emergency needs are being met by you now! I am open to receiving the abundance that is my spiritual entitlement. Thank you!'

Gaining Insight

'Thank you, Archangel Uriel, for shining your torch of light over my finances so that I may understand where I must improve or heal. Thank you for guiding my intelligence toward abundant ideas and insights. And so it is!'

Increasing

'Divine angels of abundance, thank you for circling around my financial wellbeing and for guiding me to the abundance I deserve. My income increases as I realize that it is my spiritual right to be supported. And so it is!'

Investments

'Thank you, angels, for lovingly guiding this business venture so that I know my investments are for my highest good! I surrender the direction of this situation to you. And so it is!'

Looking After

'Thank you, angels, for pouring your love over my finances. I release any fears regarding them, knowing they are looked after by your heavenly eyes!'

Focus

Avoiding Distraction

'Thank you, angels, for supporting my focus at this time. I allow myself to dedicate my time and energy to this situation, knowing it will be for my highest good! And so it is!'

Support with a Project

'Dear angels of inspiration, thank you for supporting me with this project and for allowing me to express my creativity. I know that with your direction I am the best I can be! And so it is!'

Food

Having Enough

'Dear angels, thank you for supporting me in having enough supplies. I know there is always more than enough! And so it is!'

Improving Diet

'Dear Archangel Raphael and angels of health, thank you for supporting me in choosing foods that will support the health of my body. Thank you, dear angels, for guiding me to a diet that allows me to be wholly fulfilled. And so it is!'

Forgiveness

Forgiving an Abuser

This may take some time, but the angels will support you.

'Dear angels of forgiveness, thank you for healing me as I release this past situation as an illusion, remembering that only love is real. Thank you for blessing all those involved and for lovingly guiding me to safety. I now know that I am safe and guided by you and by love! And so it is!'

Forgiving a Child

'Dear angels, thank you for allowing me to see the innocence of this child and to fully forgive. Thank you for guiding us all to a loving safe place where we can heal and let go of any issues that no longer serve us! And so it is!'

Forgiving a Parent

'Dear angels, thank you for helping me see that my parents are children of God who are doing the best they can, even though they may not have made the best decisions in the past. I love and forgive them and send them blessings so that they can see that only love is real. And so it is!'

Forgiving Everyone Involved in a Situation

'I forgive and am forgiven as I release this situation to heaven. Thank you, angels, for removing the energy that binds me to it as I set myself free! And so it is!'

(See also Archangels Jeremiel and Zadkiel.)

Freedom

'Angels of light, thank you for guiding me as I leap into my own space and freedom. I know I am always safe and protected by you. It feels so good to be alive! And so it is!'

G

Goals

Achieving

'Dear angels, thank you for supporting me as I focus on this goal. I am so passionate about this subject and feel so thrilled knowing I have achieved my dreams. It feels amazing knowing I constantly achieve more and more. And so it is!'

Setting

'Thank you, Archangel Uriel, for filling me with inspiration and light as I set my goals for the time ahead. I know with your support, anything is possible!'

Grace

'Divine angels of grace, thank you for filling my soul with your light so that I can view all the situations of my life with clarity and compassion. I now begin to live with mercy and grace as I stand tall, confident and safe in your light. And so it is!'

Grieving

Archangel Azrael, the angel of transition, will comfort and heal the hearts of those who are feeling left behind or at a loss.

Healing the Heart

'Thank you, Archangel Azrael and angels, for surrounding me in your healing light. I allow my heart to heal as I remember there is no separation between heaven and Earth. I know my loved ones are the wings that take me forward. And so it is!'

Sending Healing to Someone in Need

'Thank you, Archangel Azrael and healing angels, for circling around [name of person] *in this time of need. Thank you for guiding them to a safe*

and loved place. I pray in the Law of Grace and surrender this to you. And so it is!'

Grounding Yourself

Ensure your spine is erect and both your feet are on the ground with this prayer:

'Dear angels of the Earth, with both of my feet on the ground and my spine erect, I allow my spiritual energy to connect with every major organ of my body. I allow any extra energy to go into the planet to heal it. I now allow cords of light to come from my feet and to penetrate the Earth as they anchor me into the ground, providing safety and stability. I am grounded, I am earthed, I am safe and strong. And so it is!'

H

Happiness

Encouraging

'Thank you, angels of joy and light, for reminding me of your presence. Thank you for helping me see the joy and blessings in my life. I feel so happy and abundant knowing that the life I want is here! And so it is!'

Praying for Someone Else's Happiness

'Dear angels of joy and light, thank you for filling [name]'s life with your energy and presence. Thank

you for reminding them of the joy they are, of the gifts they have, and of the light they hold within. I surrender this to you in the Law of Grace. And so it is!'

Healing and Health

Archangel Raphael, the healing angel, will support all calls for health and healing. He is the divine physician working directly with God.

Accepting Health and Healing

'Dear Archangel Raphael and angels, I accept health now. Knowing that my body is safe, that my immune system is strong and that my blood flows beautifully around my body is absolutely perfect. All my major organs are filled with angelic healing light as I affirm my body is whole. I am healed, I am well and healthy! And so it is!'

Hands-on Healing

'Thank you, angels of healing light, for supporting my natural healing abilities as I put my hands on [name of client] *to support their health and wellbeing. They are well, they are healed. And so it is!'*

Sending Healing

'Thank you, healing angels, for surrounding [name of person] *in your light and for supporting their path to wellbeing. I pray to you under the Law of*

Grace, knowing you will do the best for them, their journey and the growth of their soul. And so it is!'

Home

Blessing Your Home

'Divine angels of serenity, thank you for washing your wave of light over and through my home. The space is positive, clear and safe, with love flowing freely within. My home is blessed and full of abundance! And so it is!'

Finding the Perfect Home

'Thank you, Archangel Jophiel and angels, for lovingly guiding me to the perfect home for my family's needs! And so it is!'

I

Inspiration

'Thank you, Archangel Uriel and dear angels of light, for inspiring me to see my inner gifts and talents so I may share them with the world. It feels so good to share! And so it is!'

Integrity

'Thank you, Archangel Gabriel and angels of honesty, for standing by me as I speak my truth with integrity. I know that the truth is the best gift I can offer in this situation, and I open my heart with humility. And so it is!'

Intuition

'Thank you, angels of divine guidance, for unlocking my intuition so that I can trust the source of divine inspiration that constantly flows through me! And so it is!'

J
Job

(See Career.)

Justice

If you're seeking justice in a particular situation, surrender it to Archangel Zadkiel, who will bring about balance for you.

'Dear Zadkiel, angel of God, I surrender this situation to you, knowing that you will bring balance and compassion to it. Thank you for taking control. And so it is!'

L
Leadership

'Thank you, angels, for allowing me to stand on my own two feet and for leading the way to love. I know that I can be the change I want to see in the world; thank you for bringing me the courage I need to serve this purpose. I know you want nothing more than happiness for me, and I allow you to guide me. And so it is!'

Legal Matters

In situations that are very serious, allow God to take over. He and his divine angels will support you.

'Dear angels, I surrender this legal situation to you, knowing that the light of mercy, compassion and righteousness washes over it. I allow God to take control and know all that happens is for the highest good of all involved. I know I am always safe in God's arms. And so it is!'

Life Purpose

'Divine angels, thank you for supporting me as I remember and serve my purpose. I just love living a life of service! And so it is!'

(See also Archangel Chamuel.)

Lost Items

'Thank you, Archangel Sandalphon, for lovingly guiding me to [lost item] using my dreams and intuition. I know I will feel inspired to find it again by your amazing light! And so it is!'

Love

'Dear angels of love, thank you for filling my heart with your divine essence so that I can see, hear and experience love everywhere I go! God is a part of me, and as I see the love within, it reflects

outwards in my life. Life is just so tremendous and I am love itself. And so it is!'

M
Manifestation

'Dear Archangel Raziel and angels of abundance, thank you for supporting me in manifesting the life I love and deserve. I know God constantly supports me and it feels absolutely amazing! I step back and allow the divine will to guide me! And so it is!'

Marriage

(See Relationships.)

Meditation

'Dear angels, thank you for joining me in my meditation practice and for inspiring me with your light. I know when I take the time to listen through meditation, your guidance is always clearly given to me. And so it is!'

Mercy

(See Archangel Zadkiel and Forgiveness.)

Miracles

'Thank you, heaven, I hand this situation to you, knowing that as I focus on love the miracle begins to unfold. And so it is!'

(See also Archangel Jeremiel.)

Money

(See Abundance or Finances.)

Motivation

'Thank you, angels, for motivating me to see the potential I have to offer this amazing life and planet. I feel inspired and energized by your presence alone! And so it is!'

Music

Archangel Sandalphon, the master of song, will help you connect to the energy of music for writing and performing alike.

'Dear Archangel Sandalphon and angels of song, thank you for blessing me with your presence and supporting me as I open up my creative heart and channel my inner musician! I feel totally uplifted knowing you are dancing by my side! And so it is!'

O

Organization

'Thank you, Archangel Jophiel, for clearing the clutter in my mind so that I can take control of my life and schedule. It feels wonderful to be organized and prepared. I trust that only good things are before me and I am always ready for them! And so it is!'

P

Passion

'Thank you, angels of spiritual passion, for blessing my life with your light as I find and focus on the blessings in my life that fulfil my every need. I am a passionate spiritual being, creating and expressing passion at every opportunity! And so it is!'

Peace

'Dear angels of peace, thank you for blessing my world and the universe so that we can remember the most important lesson: that only love is real! I feel so blessed to know this truth! And so it is!'

Pregnancy

'Thank you, Archangel Gabriel and angels, for supporting me in creating the perfect healthy child I deserve. I am overjoyed to be a woman and to create life on this planet. I am happy, healthy and abundant. And so it is!'

(See also Archangel Gabriel; Children.)

Promotion

(See Career.)

Protection

'Thank you, Archangel Michael, for surrounding me in your gentle blue light of protection. I know I am safe when you are near! And so it is!'

Psychic Abilities

Opening Up

'Dear angels, thank you for opening up my spiritual awareness so I can become aware of who and what surrounds me. I now open my third eye to perceive clearly love and wisdom from heaven in the name of the Holy Spirit. And so it is!'

Closing Down

'Thank you, God and angels, for all that has been received. I ask that any leftover energy surrounding me be taken into the universe and used wherever needed. I say this in the Law of Grace as I now close down my third eye and relax. And so it is!'

R

Relationships

Chamuel is the angel of love, and Raphael can bring a relationship healing and support. When things go 'wrong', Raguel and Zadkiel can create peace, harmony and forgiveness.

Allowing Yourself to Trust

'Thank you, Archangels Chamuel and Raphael,
for supporting me as I open my heart to receive
the love I deserve and for helping me to discern
when I should allow myself to trust. I surrender my
relationship status to God and allow him lovingly
to guide me! And so it is!'

Connecting with a Twin Flame

'Thank you, angels, for helping me recognize,
understand and connect with my twin flame so that
I can learn and grow even more in life. I surrender
this to you. And so it is!'

Finding a Soul Mate

'Thank you, Archangel Chamuel, for lovingly
guiding me to my soul-mate relationship so I
can receive the love I deserve. I now open my
heart to passion, fulfilment and love. I am open
to receiving!'

Harmony and Healing

'Thank you, Archangels Raguel and Raphael, for
surrounding our relationship in a space of serene
love. I love my partner very much and allow you
to direct us to a place where we can open up with
honesty and humility. Our love alone will guide us
through this time, but with your help I know that
miracles are possible. And so it is!'

Strengthening a Relationship

Dear Archangel Michael, Archangel Chamuel
and angels, thank you for pouring your strength
and light into our relationship and guiding us to a
balanced space in mind, body and soul! And so it is!

(See also Divorce; Romance.)

Romance

'Angels of romance, I surrender my love life to you,
knowing you are blessing my energy with love.
Thank you for the increasing romance in my life,
as the more I experience, the more I love myself!
And so it is!'

S

Self-Esteem

Say this prayer while wrapping your arms around
yourself in a comforting way:

'Graceful angels of God, thank you for supporting
me in discovering my amazing self. I am overjoyed
to strengthen my connection with myself!'

Sexuality

'Divine angels of God, thank you for allowing me
to lovingly accept myself and acknowledge my
sexuality. This is a true and spiritual part of myself
that I now see and acknowledge. It feels so good to
be filled with joy and passion for life! And so it is!'

Sleep

'Angels of love and serenity, thank you for surrounding me as I allow myself to flow into a deep relaxed sleep. I am safe and protected by your light. And so it is!'

Spiritual Growth

'Angels of light, thank you for illuminating the path to my spiritual growth. Increasing my connection and faith is my focus.'

Strength

'Thank you, Archangel Michael, for allowing me to tap into the spiritual strength that supports me in all areas of my life. My feet are earthed and grounded in safety!'

Switching Off (Tuning Out)

'Thank you, angels, for disconnecting my energy from any outside source as I relax and go within. I am safe and free!'

T

Teaching

For Support in Sharing your Knowledge

'Thank you, angels, for supporting me as I pass on the knowledge I have learned to others. I know there is more than enough knowledge in this world

for everyone and trust that you will help me in explaining what I know to the best of my ability. It brings me great joy to share my truth with all of those willing to learn and grow. I am willing to serve! And so it is!'

For Teachers

'Divine angels of knowledge, thank you for blessing my classroom with your serene light. I know that this space is a reflection of what I feel within, so I take a deep breath and breathe out peaceful and relaxed thoughts. I thank Archangel Gabriel for helping me speak with clarity and Archangel Haniel for helping me stand with grace and poise. I feel absolutely overjoyed at sharing my work with these young souls who are constantly growing and developing. Thank you, dear God, for guiding my day. I know it's going to be great! And so it is!'

Time

'Thank you, Archangel Metatron, for supporting me in being on time as I recognize what my true priorities are. I know that my day always runs according to divine timing! And so it is!'

Travel

'Thank you, Archangels Raphael and Michael, for safely guiding me on my journey today. I know

that it's going to be a breath of fresh air as your wings envelop me in protection, comfort and love. And so it is!'

Truth

(See Integrity.)

W

Weight Loss

'Thank you, angels, for blessing my body. It's such a beautiful and safe place to be. It feels so amazing letting go of the pounds I no longer need. And so it is!'

Writing

(See Creativity.)

Y

Yoga

'Thank you, Archangel Raziel, for supporting me as I tap into the knowledge and wisdom contained within yoga. I know as I connect with my body I allow my mind and soul to grow, too. Thank you for inspiring me to adapt, and to learn to breathe and pose with ease. And so it is!'

∽ RECOMMENDED READING ∽

A Course in Miracles (Foundation for Inner Peace, Inc., 1975)

Gabrielle Bernstein, *Spirit Junkie* (Hay House UK, 2011)

Louise Hay, *You Can Heal Your Life* (Hay House, 1984)

Anodea Judith, *Chakra Balancing* (Sounds True Inc., 2004)

Caroline Myss, *Anatomy of Spirit* (Bantam 1997)

Doreen Virtue, *The Lightworker's Way* (Hay House, 1997) and *Chakra Clearing* (Hay House, 2004)

Marianne Williamson, *A Return to Love* (HarperCollins, 1992)

ABOUT THE AUTHOR

Kyle Gray is an angel communicator, medium and motivational speaker based in the west of Scotland where he was born and raised. He has a weekly column in *The Scottish Sun* newspaper and a monthly column in *Spirit & Destiny* magazine where he shares his experiences and guidance from the angels.

The world as Kyle knew it changed at the age of four when his beloved grandmother passed away and visited him from the other side. With an increased sensitivity to feel spirits, it was destined that Kyle would pursue a career as a medium and angel communicator. After his first angel experience at the age of 15, Kyle's interest and talents developed quickly, and he was named 'The Youngest Medium in the UK' at just 17 years of age.

Kyle now travels widely to spread the love and guidance from the angels. With his effervescent character and upfront, rock-and-roll approach, Kyle warms the hearts of those he meets. While he is relatively young for the job he is doing, Kyle's knowledge of spirituality goes beyond his years, and his enthusiasm and energy lend the subject of angels a new light.

Kyle is based in Glasgow, Scotland, where he gives readings and coaches clients to create change, heal old wounds and connect with the other side.

http://kylegray.co.uk
http://twitter.com/MGCK
http://facebook.com/kylegrayuk